STRATEGIC WOMEN

Scottish Women's Studies Series

A GUID CAUSE
Women's Suffrage Movement in Scotland
Leah Leneman

MARRIAGE AND PROPERTY
Elizabeth Craik (ed)

KATHARINE ATHOLL 1874-1960
Sheila Hetherington

BAJANÉLLAS AND SEMILINAS:
Aberdeen University and the Education of Women 1860-1920
Lindy Moore

UPSTAIRS TO DOWNSTAIRS
Advice to Servant Girls and Weary Mothers
James Drummond (ed)

SCOTTISH WOMEN'S STUDIES SERIES

Strategic Women

How do they manage — in Scotland? —

Elisabeth Gerver & Lesley Hart

ABERDEEN UNIVERSITY PRESS

First published 1991
Aberdeen University Press

British Library Cataloguing in Publication Data

A catalogue record for this book is available from the British Library.

ISBN 0 08 037741 6

Typeset by BEECEE Typesetting Services
Printed by Athenaeum Press Ltd, Newcastle-upon-Tyne

To Miriam and Laura

Contents

Acknowledgements

This book is the result of a great deal of help and advice from many people. Firstly, we should like to thank Ethel Gray, Esther Roberton and Olga Wojtas for their frank, imaginative and helpful suggestions about the names of possible interviewees. Secondly, we should like warmly to thank the forty-eight women who gave their time and thought to answering Lesley's detailed questions; their openness and candour have made this book possible.

We also appreciate Margaret MacIntosh's suggestions about illustrations. We are grateful to Martine Beattie and Ann McNaught for their help with the development of the database, their analysis of some of the data and their help in word-processing at various stages.

We acknowledge gratefully the others who have willingly given us information, advice or help in other ways with the book: Alan and Morag Alexander, Caroline Bamford, Lalage Bown, Sheena Briley, Alice Brown, Sally Brown, Elizabeth Bryan, Elizabeth Campbell, Dawn Corbett, Mark Cox, Carol Craig, Judith George, Alexander Gerver, Leslie Hills, Hope Johnston, Christine McBain, Irene Macpherson, Ron Miller, Arlene Nunnery, Gill Scott, Caroline Slater, Anne Sturrock, Margaret Sutherland, Katrina Tompkins, Margaret Walsh, the statistics division of the Scottish Education Department and the members of Network in Scotland.

We should like to thank the following for permission to use copyright material: Jackie Fleming, Leeds Postcards, Viv Quillan, Leonie Still and *The Times Higher Education Supplement*.

We also very much appreciate the tolerance shown by our families during the many hours when Lesley was away conducting interviews, when Elisabeth was hidden in her attic study at her word-processor, and when we were both engrossed with the analysis.

The book is dedicated to our daughters, Miriam Gerver and Laura Hart. We hope that their public and private lives in the twenty-first century will bring them the sense of fulfilment experienced by many of the women whose living strategies appear on the following pages.

University of Dundee and
University of Strathclyde

Introduction

This book was conceived at a moment when, during a presentation to urge Scottish employers to take more seriously the potential of women for senior posts in industry, we were struck by the apparent disjunction of trends relating to education and employment in Scotland. The Scottish education system has rightly taken pride in the opportunities available to both boys and girls over many years. In recent years, both Scottish girls and boys have been leaving school more highly qualified than ever before — indeed the level of educational qualifications held now by children on leaving school is double that of their parents' generation (Nelson, 1989). In particular, Scottish girls for a number of years have been leaving school more highly qualified than their brothers (Bamford, 1988).

But there appear to be strikingly few women employed in senior positions in Scotland. There seem to be even fewer, indeed, than in the rest of Britain. Yet labour force participation rates for females are slightly higher in Scotland than in Britain as a whole: the 1984 Census of Employment shows a rate of 44.2 per cent for female participation in the labour force in Scotland, as compared with 43.9 per cent for Britain as a whole. Women in Scotland also enter higher education in greater numbers than in the rest of Britain and they emerge to a greater extent with degrees of the kind that are often thought to guarantee a successful future in the industrial and professional world. While in the rest of the UK, for instance, only about 8 per cent of students entering computing science courses at universities in 1987 were female, in Scotland females formed 15 per cent of entrants to university undergraduate computer courses (MacKinlay, 1989a).

We then considered one situation in which highly educated women might be expected to be well represented — that of university academic posts. The total number of women in university academic posts in the UK as a whole was relatively small at 14 per cent in 1989 (Halsey, 1990). But, of all the groupings of universities in the UK, Scotland has the lowest proportion of female academics: overall, only 10.7 per cent of university academic staff in Scotland are female, as compared with 19 per cent

1

amongst the London group and 17.3 per cent in Oxford and Cambridge (Halsey, 1990).

The mystery for both of us was why exceptional achievement by females at school in Scotland has been tied to exceptional under-achievement in the world of work.

Our first stumbling block in trying to suggest answers was that we were uncertain about the extent of the problem. How far were our perceptions that there were few women in senior positions in Scotland true? Anecdotal evidence suggested that, at least in the fields with which we were familiar, the numbers of women in senior positions could be counted on the fingers of one hand; indeed, in many cases, on no hands at all. In Regional Councils, there were no female chief executives, and all the directors of education were male. In central government, of the twenty-four individuals in the three top tiers of the Scottish civil service in 1989, twenty-three were men. Of the seventy Scottish MPs, three were women. There were no female heads of any higher education institutions. Even in a subject studied predominantly by females, all but one of the chairs of education and continuing education at Scottish universities in 1989 were held by men.

So we tried to establish how representative our initial assessment of the problem might be. The answer was that there was no answer. The information did not exist in any coherent form because, on the whole, such questions had not generally been thought worth asking except by individuals researching specific facets of female representation (see, for instance, the studies cited in Bamford, 1988). 'There is a marked paucity of literature about women and employment in Scotland during this century' said the Women in Scotland Bibliography Group in 1988. In 1990 the Scottish Institute of Adult and Continuing Education (SIACE) found that 'there is a general dearth of statistical data on the subject of women in management in Scotland.' The only information available, from recent Labour Force Surveys, suggested that, starting from relatively low levels, the percentage of women managers in Scotland was decreasing at a time when the percentage of female managers in Britain as a whole was rising: in 1983 24.6 per cent of basic managers in Scotland were female, but by 1987 this figure had dropped to 24.2 per cent. Over the same period female basic managers in Britain as a whole rose from 24 per cent to 27 per cent (SIACE, 1990).

Other indicators suggested that we should be wrong, that the trend should be one of increasing rather than decreasing female participation in senior positions, in keeping with much of the rest of the developed world. At the beginning of the 1990s in Scotland, for instance, educational institutions in Scotland almost all claim to be 'equal opportunities employers'. During the 1970s there had been three women principals of centrally funded higher education institutions. Yet, by the beginning of the 1990s, there were only male principals.

Our second problem arose because it is notoriously more difficult to investigate why something is not so than why it is so. Such difficulties are compounded for issues as sensitive as those of gender and power. As Bamford (1988) and Gerver and Johnston (1990) have shown, gender sensitive research in Scotland is little practised. Even where questions of gender are investigated, the results may be inconclusive. For instance, the only full-scale study of women and management in Scotland (SIACE, 1990) has found that male employers and female staff tend overall to hold differing views about many issues in women's career development. Not unexpectedly, male and female perceptions are most at odds in those areas which have conventionally been regarded as most sensitive, such as the existence of old boys' networks as one factor in women's lack of career development: 72 per cent of female staff but only 32 per cent of male employers believe that 'male managers tend to operate an old boys' network'.

We were thus faced with questions which most people appeared to feel were not worth asking, for which no systematic or conclusive evidence existed, and which appeared too sensitive for any straightforward investigation. Clearly, research was needed into the current representation of women in senior positions in Scotland and the resulting data needed to be monitored over a period of years in order to identify trends. Where there is reluctance to acknowledge that a problem exists, however, there is likely to be even greater reluctance to fund any major research in the area. We therefore decided against pursuing that route, while recognising both the need and the potential benefits of such work.

Instead, we turned to the fact that we both knew, from our professional and our personal experience in Scotland, a few women who had clearly succeeded in objective, if crude, terms. They were often the first female occupants of particularly influential posts; their names tended to appear in *Who's Who in Scotland*; their keynote speeches were reported in the press; they served as Secretary of State chairmen (*sic*) or appointees to quangos or governing bodies; they had a formidable reputation for being able to make things happen, to get action on problems.

So, we decided to start near home. We invited a few friends to a supper party at which we discussed the idea of this book and asked for suggestions about possible interviewees. We considered a variety of approaches. Should we include women who exert considerable influence through their husbands? Should we try to interview the Scotswomen who are emigrating in increasingly large numbers? What about women who, without being in paid employment, make extraordinary contributions through voluntary work? What about our best artists and creative writers? What about those women whose talents, intelligence and judgement remain, as with Mrs Wilcox and Margaret Schlegel in *Howard's End*, at home, nurturing their families? And what about the men with whom most women work and live?

Because we too have families and full-time jobs, we decided even as early as that supper party that it would be impossible to interview and to analyse the resulting information about more than forty or fifty women. Should we choose interviewees who had achieved publicly recognised positions of influence, thereby enabling us to say something about the factors that seemed to shape how they achieved and how they used their power? Or should we seek out a wider range of women's experiences as a starting-point for a broader study of changing social patterns and expectations? Either way, we decided not to interview the men in the lives of our interviewees, because of lack of time to deal with the practical and the analytical problems involved.

In the end, we decided to focus on women who have achieved positions of publicly recognised influence. We hoped that an account of their experiences and characteristics, their strategies and tactics, would offer one useful starting-point to answering our question. At the very least, analysing the personal histories of such women as a group could help us to identify factors which they appear to have in common and which might be hypothesised to have contributed to their success. We also hoped that successful women would have useful insights into the interactions of influential men and women at work. At best, we believed that such women represent emerging models of how it is possible to flourish both professionally and personally in a country where there are few of their kind.

We therefore decided to interview fifty women, who were recognised by at least some of their peers as being highly successful in their professional lives, in a variety of different fields: government, industry, law, finance, medicine, education, voluntary organisations and the media. A list of their names and occupations appear in Appendix I; a copy of the letter requesting the interview forms Appendix II.

We were particularly pleased with, and very grateful for, the high level of positive response which we received. We sent out a total of seventy letters requesting interviews. The book contains the results of forty-eight interviews. We also interviewed one another, in order to check the scope, depth and relevance of our interview schedule. Because of the relatively small size of Scotland, we had some preliminary acquaintance with about ten of the interviewees.

In deciding to conduct these interviews, we were very conscious that reporting the results of interviews with successful women is a rapidly growing industry (see, for example, Mitchell, 1984; Miles, 1985; Jones,

1987; Henriques, 1988; Bryce, 1989; Watson, 1989; amongst very many others). Analysing the overall patterns of female achievement in a male-oriented world has also produced extensive comment over the past decade (see, for example, Acker and Piper, 1984; Cooper and Davidson, 1984; Game and Pringle, 1984; Beechey and Whitelegg, 1986; Dex, 1987; Jensen, Hagen and Reddy, 1988; Baines, 1988).

There has also been a substantial amount of work in many specific areas related to the professional and private experiences of senior women. Indeed, so much literature has now accumulated that, in each part of the discussion in the rest of this paragraph, we shall cite only one example drawn from very many others. Examinations of overall structural issues in women's employment in senior posts in organisations include statistical surveys of female representation in decision-making (Hansard, 1990), women's experience in male-dominated occupations (Spencer and Podmore, 1987), the effect of equal opportunities policies (SIACE, 1990) and the impact of sex role stereotypes (Bartol, 1980). Studies of strategies adoped by individual females developing their careers include the role of women's increased professional qualifications (Crompton and Sanderson, 1986), the use of mentors (Clutterbuck and Devine, 1987), and dealing with sexual harassment (Rendel, 1982). There has also been growing interest in changing managerial values (Scase and Goffee, 1989) and the emergence of so-called female styles of management (Marshall, 1984). The circumstances and attitudes of the domestic lives of professional women have been widely reported in studies of dual-career families (Rapoport and Rapoport, 1976).

Despite the plethora of books recounting interviews with senior women and the well-filled bookcases of sociological and philosophical studies of trends and issues in the experience of working women, there have been remarkably few studies which attempt to set a wider social context for material gathered from interviews with women in senior positions in a variety of occupational areas. Marshall (1984), Yeandle (1984), and Scase and Goffee (1989), amongst others, provide often penetrating analysis drawn from a well-established theoretical background. Like nearly all of the other sources cited so far, however, their assumptions, hypotheses and data are drawn from English sources. Despite its longer history of professional education of women, Scotland has not so far featured in any broadly based study of the experience of senior women.

Having decided both on the rationale for the book and on the main source of our data, we then agreed on our major divisions of labour. Because of her extensive experience of careers work, Lesley conducted all but one of the semi-structured interviews; the sole exception was the one which Elisabeth conducted with Lesley herself. Most interviews took place in the interviewee's office. The surroundings varied from cramped, even shabby premises to more comfortable and spacious settings in modern, well-equipped buildings. None of the offices could have been described as grandiose or imposing, and only those of the Lord Provosts of Glasgow and Edinburgh showed any external evidence of the interviewee's position of authority.

Lesley was always welcomed and made to feel at home. She was rarely kept waiting; on the few occasions when waiting was unavoidable, she found that the secretaries (all of whom were female) were eager to talk and to learn about the book. They all appeared to be proud of their female bosses and pleased that their achievements were to be recognised in this way.

The interviews were wide-ranging, as may be seen from the note of topics covered in Appendix III. The topics covered included personal histories up to the time of the interviewee's first paid employment, career paths, perceived connections between gender and leadership, and attitudes towards other women, including what advice they would offer to young women. Questions touched on, and even probed, often deeply sensitive and personal issues. Lesley asked about, for instance, how interviewees' career development impinged on their marriages and vice versa, how they met the often conflicting demands of their children and their professional lives, whether they had experienced sexual discrimination or harassment, what their parents' expectations of them had been, and details of their political and religious allegiances.

Lesley's fears that, given this range of depth and questioning, the interviewees might be slow or reluctant to respond, were ill founded. Very few were reticent or reserved. Usually she found that the problem was more one of drawing the interview to a close. The average length of the interviews was one and a quarter hours, with many lasting for over two hours.

Most of the interviews were conducted throughout the spring and summer of 1989, with a few being completed only early in 1990, because of the difficulty in fitting into the lives of very busy women. Because of the gap in time between the first and last of the interviews, several of our interviewees have already been promoted to even more senior positions since Lesley saw them; the list of their occupations in Appendix II includes details of their present positions as they reported them to us in 1990.

Did the women speak the truth? Did they omit crucial factors explaining their success? It is impossible to be sure. But Lesley was impressed by their openness and candour and by the very many personal intimate details which were disclosed during the interviews. She was particularly pleased with the obvious careful thought which the women had given to the questions beforehand.

After Lesley had completed her interviews, the most basic data about each interviewee — name, age group, position in family, country of upbringing, type of schools attended, further or higher education qualifications acquired, marital status, importance of religion, presence of a mentor, present occupation and family details — were entered on a database at the Continuing Education Centre, University of Strathclyde. These data then formed the basis on which most of our subsequent analyses were conducted. Both of us also analysed detailed written accounts of the interviews and agreed on the structure and approach of our material before Elisabeth wrote the first draft of our results.

As a result of our analysis in the winter of 1989 – 90, we identified the major issues which form the substance of our chapters. In the first place, we tried to set interviewees' experiences into a broader, representative context. We explored how far they might be seen as typical of women in their generations in Scotland. We also attempted to assess how far they conform to patterns and trends already established in literature about women in senior positions elsewhere in Britain. The results of these analyses appear later in this section, as well as forming part of Chapter 1, 'Gender and Achievement in Scotland'.

We then analysed in detail the factors which appear to be implicated in the significant choices which interviewees made, or which were made for them, at crucial points in their lives. We were interested, in the first place, in their experiences as girls and young women. What factors in their home backgrounds as children helped to shape their aspirations and assumptions about themselves as women? How far, as children and adolescents, did they picture themselves as potentially successful women? What did their experiences at school teach them about their expectations? How far were they committed to causes outside their immediate environment? Why did they decide to go on to higher education or to enter employment immediately after school? The results of this analysis appear in Chapter 2, 'The Cradle of Ambition'.

We then focused on the patterns of interviewees' paid employment. In particular, we were interested in the extent to which they believe that their careers have happened through strategic planning, by chance or in other ways. We tried to trace the main patterns established in their careers and to identify the major motivations at each stage. This analysis forms the basis of Chapter 3, 'Career Tapestries'.

We then considered a number of important issues related to interviewees' working modes and styles. Do they feel that they manage differently because they are women? What are their relationships with both male and female colleagues? Have they experienced sex discrimination or sexual harassment, and, if so, how have they dealt with it? Chapter 4, 'Women as Leaders', draws largely on the results of this analysis.

In preparing Chapter 5 on 'Leaders as Women', we analysed how
interviewees try to establish balance in their lives as they cope creatively
with the potential or actual conflicting demands of their domestic and
professional lives. We were particularly interested in decisions which they
have reached about marriage, children, the care of other dependents, and
the effects, if any, of the career choices of the partners of those in long-
term relationships.

Finally, in analysing material for Chapter 6, 'Nurturing the Future',
we investigated how far interviewees feel themselves responsible for the
career development of other women. We also identified common themes
and issues arising from their comments about the kind of women they
most admire or dislike and the advice which they offer to young women.

In our analysis and citing of material from these interviews, we have
tried, in keeping with our promise to the interviewees, to ensure that each
remains anonymous, so that we can report their direct and frank
comments. Wherever possible we have referred to the sources of
comments by the interviewee's field of work. Our references to these
areas of work, however, are not always uniform. Many of our
interviewees were educated or trained in one discipline or profession but
subsequently pursued their career in a very different field; one
interviewee, therefore, may at different times be described as being in law,
government, education, or a voluntary organisation. This diverse range of
ascriptions serves usefully to increase the degree of anonymity conferred,
but it also reflects one of the most important characteristics of our
interviewees, nearly all of whom have pursued tapestried careers.

In addition, many of the posts held by our interviewees could be
described variously as being in any one of a number of different fields. Is
the National Union of Students best described as a voluntary organisation,
as a union or as an institution primarily involved in education? Is the
Scottish Community Education Council to be seen primarily as an
educational organisation or as an arm of government? Moreover, our
interviewees typically hold a number of different positions of influence
simultaneously. Should an individual be described in terms of her
appointment as chairman of a major government body or in terms of her
main paid employment? Here again we have taken a convenient licence in
describing individual interviewees variously, depending on the context of
their comments.

The results of the analysis of the interviews are, we believe, broadly
representative of trends and patterns in the lives of many, if not most,
successful women in Scotland today. Our interviewees were deliberately
chosen to reflect a range of ages, with two in their twenties, five aged over
sixty, six aged between fifty and sixty, and the rest distributed almost
evenly between those in their thirties and those in their forties. The times

when they were children and adolescents thus stretched back to the 1920s and forward to the 1970s. Interviewees were also chosen to represent a wide variety of occupational areas, including both those where women have been well represented over many generations — such as education — as well as those where female presence at a professional level has only recently become visible — such as industry.

Of course, we do not claim that in every true respect our interviewees are representative of Scottish women as a whole. Most notably, they come disproportionately from families where their father's occupation placed the family within the middle rather than the working classes. Only 30 per cent of our interviewees are from working-class backgrounds, with 68 per cent from middle-class homes (one did not disclose her father's occupation). These proportions are almost precisely the reverse of the socio-economic composition of the population of Scotland as a whole. We had not, however, attempted to select our interviewees by social class background; such information emerged only during the course of their replies to our questions. Given the apparently hefty barriers against women in senior positions in Scotland, it is probably scarcely surprising that a disproportionate number of our interviewees come from fairly privileged backgrounds.

As well as being unrepresentative in terms of social class, our interviewees are also unrepresentative in their educational experiences. They are much more highly educated, and their mothers in particular are more highly educated, than might have been predicted even from their largely middle-class backgrounds. Moreover, a much higher proportion both of working-class and of middle class interviewees have attended fee paying schools as children, despite the very low proportions in Scotland of children attending such schools.

Nevertheless, other patterns in interviewees' lives lead us to believe that, while more socially privileged and more highly educated than their contemporaries, our interviewees are in some important respects reasonably representative of women in Scotland today. Most interviewees are, or have been, married. Most have been brought up in Protestant households, reflecting approximately the balance in Scotland between Protestant and Catholic. None is from a minority ethnic community, reflecting the fact that such communities in Scotland have been estimated to form less than 2 per cent of the population as a whole.

Even in such details as their mothers' employment status, interviewees appear to reflect national trends. For instance, of those whose families had lived in England during the interviewees' childhood or adolescence, mothers were more than twice as likely as their Scottish counterparts to have worked during their daughter's adolescence; this pattern is typical of the fact that, until the 1970s, substantially fewer women in Scotland than in England worked in paid employment. Further conformity with general social trends appears in interviewees' educational experiences. The majority of those from middle-class backgrounds proceeded directly from school to university, while the majority of those from working-class homes left school to take up paid employment. These patterns too are broadly characteristic of Scotland as a whole.

Since our small sample thus appears to be representative of many important characteristics of women in Scotland as a whole, we have applied both quantitative as well as qualitative methods in analysing the results of the interviews. We fully appreciate the dangers of generalising from only fifty interviews, and we have tried to qualify the analysis accordingly. But we do believe that there is more than merely anecdotal significance in what our interviewees told us about their childhood, schooling, experiences of higher and further education, marriages, relationships with their children, and, above all, their professional lives as women exploring new possibilities for themselves and their sex. The implications of what our fifty interviewees said extend beyond the private and unique experiences of individuals to suggest broader questions about how Scotland can create more humane and fulfilling lives for all its people.

Although we are both deeply committed to raising the profile of women in Scotland, we have not written this book within a theoretical feminist framework. The impetus for our work stemmed from our intellectual and emotional curiosity about factors in women's career development in Scotland. We are well aware that, just as the women have (consciously or not) edited the material given to us at the interview, so too, from the material of their lives, we could have selected information to support any one of a number of feminist theories. We are also very conscious of our own personal preference for the kinds of lives we have chosen for ourselves — lives in which we have tried for many years, sometimes precariously, to balance professional, domestic and social commitments. But, throughout the book, we have tried to be as true to the experience of our interviewees as possible, and we have tried to draw from our data only those conclusions which appear to have been justified, both qualitatively and quantitatively, by what fifty women told us.

Incidentally, despite the somewhat unusual division of labour in preparing this book, we both feel responsible for the result. The text has been discussed, queried, argued and finally agreed by both of us; we also jointly selected the illustrations. We hope that in what follows you will come to share some of the pleasure and excitement which we have felt in preparing it.

Chapter One

Gender and Achievement in Scotland

Introduction

On the basis of the available data, it is impossible to assess the interaction of gender and achievement in Scotland. As we have already mentioned, gender has rarely been recognised as an issue in research in Scotland, and much of the information required for any comprehensive account is not available. Brown (1990a) comments that 'no major resources have been committed to exploring the position of women in . . . areas of public management', while SIACE (1990) points to 'the general dearth of statistical data on . . . women in management in [the private sector in] Scotland'.

In what follows we shall draw on the few published available sources about the representation of women in the private, public and voluntary sectors in Scotland. Our focus will lie on the fields of government and education, with selected evidence about industry and law. Our reasons for being so selective are partly because it is in these fields that the most substantial evidence is available, and partly because we believe that participation trends in these areas are likely to have a significant effect on the life of the country as a whole. Where we believe that the picture can be illuminated in the light of trends elsewhere, we have included comparative data from other parts of the United Kingdom as well as from other European countries.

We are highly conscious of the gaps in both the data and the analysis. Nevertheless, since virtually all of the evidence drawn from a range of contexts points in the same general direction, we believe that the picture

below, while not comprehensive, is probably generally representative of
the extent to which women have achieved senior positions in Scotland.

For instance, there are generally close parallels between the figures
which we cite, showing that participation by women at senior levels
hovers between 0 and 5 per cent, and the assessments made by the
publishers of *Who's Who in Scotland*. Unfortunately, the 1990 – 91
edition of *Who's Who in Scotland* was published too late for us to include
the results in this study. The 1988 – 89 edition contains 4,796 entries of
men and women. According to the dust jacket, the scope of the
publication includes 'people of achievement and influence from all
sections of Scottish society. Represented in the book are leading figures in
politics, law, the Churches, education, business and finance, the civil
service and local government, science and medicine, the arts and sport.'
Of the entries 5.7 per cent are female. *Who's Who in Scotland* tactfully
does not specify how the choice of its entries is made. As we shall show in
more detail below, we believe that its proportion of roughly 5 per cent
seems to hold true generally of the level of participation by women in
more senior positions in Scotland.

In what follows, we are defining senior positions as being the top three
or four levels of decision-making in institutions or organisations. In a
university, for instance, the senior positions would include the principal,
vice-principal, deans and professors. Amongst the elected members of a
regional council, the senior positions would include the convener and
vice-convener of the council and the conveners of major committees. In
industry, the term would include the chief executive, the level of
responsibility immediately below (almost invariably) him, and the heads of
the major departments.

If we had restricted the definition of senior positions to individuals at
the very top of major organs of government, industry and the professions,
the level of female representation would almost certainly plummet to less
than 1 per cent. There are, for instance, no female ministers in the
Scottish Office, no female principals of higher education institutions and
no female supreme court judges. There is only one female local authority
chief executive — of a small rural district council. Because we could not
have found fifty women at such levels in Scotland, therefore, we decided
to adopt the looser criterion of the top three or four levels of decision
making. It is this definition which is used throughout the discussion
which follows.

Government

At the important levels of decision-making in political life in Scotland —
the members of parliament from whom government ministers are drawn

— women are scarce, forming only 4.2 per cent of MPs from Scottish constituencies. As the table below shows, female participation is relatively low elsewhere in both the United Kingdom as a whole and much of the rest of Europe. Scotland's proportion is the worst amongst first chambers.

WOMEN MEMBERS OF PARLIAMENTS IN THE EUROPEAN COMMUNITY :
NATIONAL PARLIAMENTS JAN 1989 AND EUROPEAN PARLIAMENT SEPT 1989

Member State	Parliament	No. of Females	Total Members	Females as % of Total	Year of Election
Danmark	Folketing	55	179	30.7	1988
Nederland	Tweede Kamer	32	150	21.3	1986
Nederland	Eerste Kamer	16	75	21.3	1987
European Community	European Parliament	98	518	18.9	1984
Deutschland	Bundestag	83	519	16.0	1987
Deutschland*	Länderregierungen	18	134	13.4	1988
Italia	Camera dei Deputati	81	630	12.9	1987
Luxembourg	Chambre des Députés	7	64	10.9	1984
Portugal	Assemblia da República	25	250	10.0	1987
Belglë/ Belgique	Ch des Représentants	18	212	8.5	1987
Ireland	Dáil Éireann	14	166	8.4	1987
Ireland	Seanad Éireann	5	60	8.3	1987
Belglë/ Belgique	Sénat	15	183	8.2	1987
España	Congreso/Diputados	27	345	7.8	1986
United Kingdom	House of Commons	42	650	6.5	1987
Italia	Senato della Repubblica	20	315	6.3	1987
España	Senado	15	253	5.9	1986
France	Assemblée Nationale	33	577	5.7	1988
United Kingdom	House of Lords	66	1,187	5.6	—
Ellas	Vouli ton Ellinon	13	300	4.3	1985
France	Sénat	8	319	2.5	1986

* This figure refers to the members of the regional (Land) governments, and not to the second chamber — the Bundesrat — which only comprises 45 members.

(Commission of the European Communities, 1989)

Because the numbers of women MPs in Scotland are so small and perhaps because there are no women Conservative MPs in Scotland, there are no women ministers in the Scottish Office. Within the civil service supporting the government, in 1989 there was only one woman amongst the top twenty-four posts. Females are rather better represented amongst that part of the Scottish establishment which is composed of the chairmen (*sic*) of organisations whose board members and trustees are appointed by the Secretary of State for Scotland. Of Scottish Office appointments to public bodies, 20 per cent are female, and 10 per cent of such public bodies have women in the chair (Nelson, 1988).

Amongst elected members of local government in Scotland, the figures for female participation are much higher, although still substantially lower than in several European parliaments: 18 per cent of elected councillors in Scotland are female (Scottish Local Government Information Unit, 1989). There are, correspondingly, a number of elected women members at the heads of councils in Scotland, including, in 1990, the president of the Convention of Scottish Local Authorities. There are also growing numbers of women amongst the lower tiers of senior management in local authorities, such as at the level of depute and assistant directors in council departments.

At district council level, the situation of Stirling District may share important features with other local authorities. While we cannot trace any analysis of the male:female balance specifically for the top three or four levels of decision-making, Stirling District has published the results of a study which indicates that women are disproportionately concentrated in the lower salary ranges and under-represented in the higher, as the following figure shows:

Figure 2

WOMEN AND MEN AS A PERCENTAGE OF THE TOTAL WORKFORCE
EMPLOYED WITHIN EACH SALARY RANGE

Spinal Column Points	Women as % of Total Workforce	Men as % of Total Workforce	Total %
1 – 14	85	15	100
15 – 23	60	40	100
24 – 30	28	72	100
31 – 35	26	74	100
36 +	12	88	100

(Stirling District Council, 1989)

A roughly similar pattern emerges for Glasgow District Council:

Figure 3

CHANGE IN GENDER COMPOSITION OF EMPLOYEES 1982 – 9

| Salary Point | Females As % of All Employees | | | Variance | Males Variance |
	1982	1984	1989	1984-9	1984-9
1 – 15	69.6	67.5	67.8	+ 37	+ 7
16 – 22	42.0	41.5	50.4	+ 135	—45
23 – 35	15.7	18.8	24.1	+ 148	+ 89
36 – 45	6.4	7.5	10.3	+ 27	+ 90
46 – 58	4.7	6.0	11.2	+ 17	+ 49
59 – 65	0.0	0.0	0.0	nil	—6

(Glasgow District Council,
Equal Opportunities Report 1984 and 1989, computerised records)

At both elected and officer level in central and local government in Scotland, then, women are substantially under-represented, although they appear in somewhat greater numbers in quangos and advisory bodies. Throughout, the trend appears to be towards both vertical and horizontal segregation of the sexes, with women concentrated at lower levels and in particular fields. How far does such a pattern hold true of the world of education?

Education

At all three levels — primary, secondary and tertiary — of Scottish education, male:female participation of students and pupils is overall roughly equal (Bamford, 1988). More detailed analysis shows considerable variation in subjects and levels of courses. At Ordinary grade,

Figure 4

GENDER AND EXAMINATIONS

(Scottish Examination Board Report for 1986 — Table 2(a) SED, 1987)

for instance, there is a noticeable tendency for boys and girls to take qualifications in very different subjects, with the exception of English and mathematics, as shown in Figure 4.

There are relatively small differences between the numbers of male and female students at universities, centrally funded colleges and further education colleges. At post-graduate level, however, more major differences begin to emerge. In Scottish universities, 31 per cent of full-time post-graduate students were female in 1988, as contrasted with 35 per cent in UK universities as a whole; in the same year women represented 33 per cent of part-time graduate students in Scottish universities (Scottish Education Department (SED), 1990).

More striking variations between males and females appear in analysis of the gender balance of staff at Scottish universities, as the following table shows:

Figure 5

PROPORTIONS OF WOMEN AMONG STAFF AND STUDENTS OF SCOTTISH UNIVERSITIES (SPRING 1989)

	%
Members of University Courts	7
Principals in Scottish Universities	0
Professors in Scottish Universities	>3
Lecturers in Scottish Universities	10
Researchers in Scottish Universities	35
Postgraduates in Scottish Universities	31
Undergraduates in Scottish Universities	46

(Brown, 1990(a))

To focus on a single university, Fowler's (1989) study of female representation at the University of Glasgow noted the following pattern:

3 women amongst the 24 members of Court

5 women among the 121 members of Senate

8 per cent of women among the approximately 550 academics at senior lecturer level or above.

The proportion of women as senior managers within central and local government funded education bodies in Scotland is also generally low:

Figure 6

THE PROPORTION OF WOMEN AMONG SENIOR MANAGERS
IN EDUCATION (SPRING 1989)

Local Authorities	
Directors of Education	None
Depute Directors of Education	None
Assistant Directors of Education	Less than 1 in 6
Scottish Education Department	
Chief HMIs and above	None
HMIs	About 1 in 8
Assistant Secretaries and above with responsibility for education divisions	None
Scottish Examination Board	
Director and senior officers	None
Teacher Education	
College Principals	None
Professors of Education	None
Education Councils	
Chairs of Councils	2 out of 5
Directors of Councils	2 out of 5

(Brown, 1990(a))

This last table, however, presents an overtly bleak picture. Since the table was compiled, Dr Sally Brown, the author of the table, has herself been appointed as professor of education at the University of Stirling, while a woman has also been appointed as a depute director of education. Moreover, the directorships of the Scottish Council for Research in Education, the Scottish Institute of Adult and Continuing Education and the Scottish Community Education Council all passed in 1990 from three women to three other women. In local authority-supported education, however, female participation in senior posts remains extremely low, as may be seen from figures for the proportion of female staff in one local authority community education service in 1989:

Figure 7

THE PROPORTION OF MEN AND WOMEN IN COMMUNITY EDUCATION
POSTS IN ONE LOCAL AUTHORITY (SPRING 1989)

	Women	Men
1 x Education Officer	0	1
1 x Principal Community Education Officer	0	1
3 x Assistant Principal Community Education Officer	0	3
7 x Area Community Education Worker	0	7
25 x Senior Community Education Worker	3	32
Community Education Workers	56%	44%

(Brown, 1990(a))

At first glance, the Scottish figures for HM Inspectorate who are female look rather more encouraging at 10.4 per cent (Commission of the European Communities, 1989). As the following table shows, however, Scotland is second from the bottom of the league table for school inspectors, followed only by Denmark, where gender is also rarely acknowledged as an issue in education:

Figure 8

SCHOOL INSPECTORS*

Member State	Females	Males	Total	Females as % of Total
Belgique (F)	43	155	198	21.7
België (VL)	85	427	512	16.6
Danmark	88	1,989	2,077	4.2
Ellas	48	373	421	11.4
España	232	437	669	34.7
France	690	2,284	2,974	23.2
Ireland	27	160	187	14.4
Italia	80	441	521	15.4
Luxembourg	3	12	15	20.0
Nederland	—	—	—	16.0
Portugal	67	127	194	34.5
United Kingdom (E + W)	—	—	—	23.0
United Kingdom (Sc)	12	103	115	10.4

* Years: 1985/86: B, E, F, IRL, I, L, P; 1984/85: DK, GR, UK (Scotland);
  1983/84: NL, UK (England + Wales). Northern Ireland not available

(Commission of the European Communities, 1989)

The same pattern recurs for female heads of secondary school in Scotland when it is compared with its partners in the European Community. As the following table shows, Scotland is again second from the bottom, followed only by the Netherlands, where far fewer numbers of women work full time:

Figure 9

HEADS OF SECONDARY SCHOOLS

Member State	Females	Males	Total	Females as % of Total
Belgique (F)	243	538	781	31.1
België (VL)	441	1,153	1,594	27.7
Danmark	10	141	151	6.6
Ellas	982	1,275	2,257	43.5
España	274	1,129	1,403	19.5
France	1,601	5,248	6,849	23.4
Ireland	286	526	812	35.2
Italia	2,511	6,590	9,101	27.6
Luxembourg	2	22	24	8.3
Nederland	27	1,355	1,382	2.0
Portugal	61	199	260	23.5
United Kingdom (E + W)	780	4,187	4,967	15.7
United Kingdom (Sc)	15	409	424	3.5

(Commission of the European Communities, 1989)

Other professional employment

In those few specific samples of industry in which gender has been examined as a variable in employment levels in Scotland — particularly in engineering and banking, insurance and finance — women also appear to be substantially under-represented at senior levels. We are not aware of evidence about the proportion of women at senior levels in management in industry as a whole in Scotland. At all levels of management, females form about 24.2 per cent of managers in Scotland, as compared with 27 per cent in Britain as a whole (SIACE, 1990). Looking at one specific example drawn from banking, we can see in the following table that, in the Royal Bank of Scotland in 1990, there were no female branch managers in Scotland other than in Edinburgh. Scottish figures are even lower than those elsewhere in the United Kingdom:

Figure 10
THE ROYAL BANK OF SCOTLAND
FEMALES AS % OF MANAGERS AND ASSISTANT MANAGERS

	Branches	Other	Total
Managers	0.9	4.9	2.6
Assistant Managers	15.0	29.3	22.4

	UK Branches				
	Aberdeen	Edinburgh	Glasgow	London	Manchester
Managers	—	1.2	—	1.5	1.0
Assistant Managers	6.5	10.1	14.0	20.8	14.2

(Mosson, 1990)

In 1990 there were no women in the Royal Bank at executive or senior management level, although the intake of women into lower levels of management has been increasing recently, as the following figure shows:

Figure 11
THE ROYAL BANK OF SCOTLAND
FEMALE STAFF AS % OF TOTAL STAFF

	1985	1989	1990 (May)
Executive	—	—	—
Senior Management	—	—	—
Management	0.6	2.5	2.6
Assistant Management	14.0	22.0	22.4
Senior Clerical	34.9	47.4	48.6
Clerical	66.2	66.9	67.7
Secretarial	99.8	99.9	99.9
Part-time	99.3	99.4	99.4

(Mosson, 1990)

These proportions are lower than those in non-Scottish banks in the United Kingdom: even in 1984, for instance, women formed 2.8 per cent of the total of managers at Barclays Bank.

In the legal profession, much the same picture emerges. In 1990 only one Queen's Counsel in Scotland was female, while only four full-time sheriffs were women. One High Court prosecutor was female, but there were no female supreme court judges. Meanwhile, below the top levels, female participation is increasingly dramatically. In 1972, for instance, women formed only 8 per cent of solicitors, while by 1987 the proportion had risen to 24 per cent (Robertson, 1989).

Any further citing of figures — even if they were readily available — would become wearisome because the tendencies would probably be so repetitive. It is clear that, with minor variations, women are increasingly well represented at lower levels in most professional and managerial employment in Scotland. They are present in very small numbers at senior levels and scarcely ever appear at the very top. This pattern seems to be a much more extreme variant of a common pattern elsewhere in the United Kingdom and in other European countries. Why? How far are specifically Scottish factors at work? Our first step in trying to answer this question was to ask our interviewees for their assessments. In the view of these women who have survived it, how harsh a climate does Scotland present to women who aspire to senior positions?

Survivors' views

The fifty women we interviewed have survived and, indeed, flourished in their professional lives in Scotland. Many of their views, however, are unlikely to be shared by women who have aspired to more senior positions but failed to reach them: SIACE (1990) has shown clearly that aspirant female managers in Scotland hold attitudes, particularly about equal opportunities in their working environments, which differ substantially from those of women who have been promoted to management positions. Nor are the attitudes of our interviewees likely to be shared overall by those women who believe in fulfilment primarily in private rather than in public life and who would therefore not aspire to senior positions in the first place. Our interviewees are also likely to differ considerably in their views from those many women who, given the circumstances of their lives, do not even hope for any kind of personal power in their wider communities.

Nevertheless, unrepresentative though they may be of women as a whole in Scotland, our interviewees have been for many years in positions in which they could assess at first hand the attitudes of a wide range of both men and women towards living and working in Scotland. So how do our interviewees feel about Scotland? How conscious are they of the striking imbalance between the numbers of men and women in public life? How far do they feel that Scotland has offered them — and other women — a favourable environment in which to develop their careers? We attempted to answer these questions through asking those of our interviewees who had worked or lived outwith Scotland whether they felt that there are intrinsically Scottish factors which affect women's career paths. Because the resulting data cover only twenty-three interviews, we are unable to draw any firm conclusions. Nevertheless, several important characteristics of Scottish attitudes do appear to emerge from our interviewees' response to the question.

In the first place, three interviewees comment on what they see as the positive cultural and historical advantages for women of working in Scotland:

> Scotland is a good place for women to work. Scots generally are individualistic, and this helps women, who also can do very well on an individual basis. The structures are, perhaps, slightly more old-fashioned in Scotland, but there is more flexibility than down south.

> One third of district councillors in Edinburgh are women; this is a fairly high percentage. There has been a history of women working in Edinburgh, which has helped women come forward into work and into politics.

> You have to *prove* that you're not a daft wee lassie. Once you've proved this, there's usually no problem . . . I find it easier in Scotland dealing with men.

Another interviewee feels that there is little difference between Scotland and elsewhere:

> Male attitudes are not any worse in Scotland than elsewhere. Men are often blind to women's needs.'

One interviewee believes that there are geographical advantages but cultural disadvantages of working as a woman in Scotland:

> In some ways it's easier for a woman, in some ways more difficult, in Scotland. It's easier because Scotland is a small country and it's much easier to set up networks of colleagues and have a sense of sisterhood. It's more difficult because Scottish male chauvinism is much stronger than in England.

But these favourable assessments of Scotland as a working environment for women are greatly outweighed by harsher views. Eighteen interviewees, of the twenty-three for whom we have data, believe, with varying degrees of intensity, that Scotland offers a predominantly hostile climate for women in senior positions. In the first place, interviewees remark on the relative paucity of women in positions equivalent to their own in Scotland:

When I first moved to Scotland I was astonished at how few women there were in senior positions. Because there were so few visible women, I kept feeling that everything I said was interpreted as coming from a woman rather than on its own merits. I realised that I had been accepted only when I was included in an otherwise all-male conversation which assumed that a particular candidate had been included in a short leet only because she was a woman rather than because she was a serious candidate. It left a bad taste in my mouth.

Scotland is definitely behind England. In frequent trips to London I meet many more senior women than I do in Scotland.

A number of our interviewees who have travelled and often worked elsewhere in Europe comment unfavourably on the differences between Scotland and other European countries in the representation of women in senior positions.

There are probably not as many opportunities [for women] in Scotland as in England or other European countries . . . I travel around Europe, and I see many more women in senior positions in other countries.

France is a much better place for women than Scotland. I saw many more women in senior positions in that country than I come across in Scotland.

From what I have seen down south and in Europe, women are further on. There is a Scottish factor at work. There are definitely still barriers in Scotland.

As our interviewees see it, however, the extent of the under-representation of women at senior level varies throughout Scotland. It appears to be most pronounced outwith Edinburgh:

Moving from Edinburgh to Dundee was a bit of a struggle. Dundee has a much smaller business community with a lack of females in senior positions as compared with Edinburgh.

The west is still fairly conventional and conservative. It's still the norm for women to work, and educationally oriented women get a good education. But in the higher echelons of industry and commerce there's still quite a lot of discrimination. In London the number of professional women is striking, but not in Glasgow. Why are we behind? There's been no need to bring women forward; there've been plenty of men so far to fill the posts.

Like some of their counterparts already cited, a number of our interviewees comment on what they see as the reasons for the under-representation of women at senior level in Scotland. Both male and female attitudes are implicated in these assessments. In particular, our interviewees cite outright male chauvinism and the low expectations of many women:

> Scotland is not a good place for a woman to work. The west of Scotland is very entrenched about the role of women; things are especially difficult there. I have a lot of English female friends. It's not coincidence that they seem to have done very well in their careers.

> In Scotland there is an east-west divide. There is a much more macho image in the west of Scotland.

> In Scotland attitudes are definitely gender-skewed. From talking to and working with men in Scotland, I've found that very often they are either suspicious of women or contemptuous of them.

> Women in Scotland . . . do seem to lack confidence and just don't believe that they can do it.

> A major cause of there being so few women in senior positions [in my company] is women's cultural background which leads them to very low career aspirations. [My part of Scotland] is still culturally chauvinistic. It is an uphill struggle for a woman. I have to prove myself and much more is expected of me than a male in a similar position. Career development is much easier in both England and other European countries as well as in the USA.

As we shall see in more detail in Chapter 6, these generally bleak assessments of the present climate in Scotland brighten when interviewees speak about how they see the future for senior women in Scotland. But the opinions of survivors about the factors involved in the present situation can offer only a partial view. Is there any more objective evidence about why so few women in Scotland achieve positions comparable to those occupied by our interviewees? In the following section we shall try to assess the current evidence about some of the factors which appear to be implicated.

Possible factors

Because issues of gender are rarely acknowledged to be important in education and employment in Scotland, evidence in this field is extremely patchy. In what follows, therefore, as well as citing specifically Scottish findings where they are available, we have also drawn on material from studies which include Scotland as an aggregated part of Britain or the United Kingdom. We have also referred occasionally to anecdotal evidence where such evidence appears to illuminate otherwise unexplained findings.

Before discussing those factors which appear to be implicated in the under-representation of women at senior level in Scotland, it is worth noting that at least three factors which one might expect to find involved do not appear to hold. Firstly, when they leave school in Scotland, women are not less but more highly qualified than men. As early as 1962, girls were gaining as many Highers passes as boys (Marshall, 1983). By 1987 girls had overtaken boys even in the highest category of qualified school leavers — those with five or more Highers (*Regional Trends*, 1989).

Secondly, in Scotland for some considerable time, roughly equal numbers of men and women have proceeded to higher education — the required condition for nearly all entry to the professional world. Even in universities, where more men than women have participated ever since women were first admitted late in the nineteenth century, the figures are now nearly equal: in 1988 – 9 women formed 45 per cent of under-graduates at Scottish universities (SED, 1990).

Finally, the rates of female participation in the labour market in Scotland very nearly approach the rates of male participation. In 1988, for instance, females formed 45.6 per cent of the civilian workforce in employment in Scotland (*Regional Trends*, 1989).

If women's educational achievements and their rates of labour market participation are roughly comparable with those of their male counterparts, what factors might be implicated in the far lower numbers of women in senior positions? However scanty, evidence from both Scottish and other sources suggests that complex, interacting factors are at work. These factors appear to fall into four main categories: historical patterns, social attitudes, employment practices and the general lack of awareness of gender as an issue.

HISTORICAL PATTERNS

As Marshall (1983) has shown, for women in Scotland as well as throughout most of the world, marriage rather than work has long been the primary means of social advancement. As Marshall depicts them through examination of evidence from mediaeval times onwards, Scottish women have been characterised by hard work, energy, humour and determination. She concludes that 'the figure of the resolute woman has been a familiar one in Scotland for centuries . . . Throughout Scottish history women have enjoyed an unusual degree of influence despite the constraints of law and convention.'

Nevertheless, the development of professional careers for women in Scotland has been, as Marshall depicts it, a 'fluctuating process'. Since women were admitted to university during the latter part of the nineteenth century, Marshall suggests, they made rapid progress in the 1920s and 1930s, with a lessening of impetus in the 1940s and 1950s,

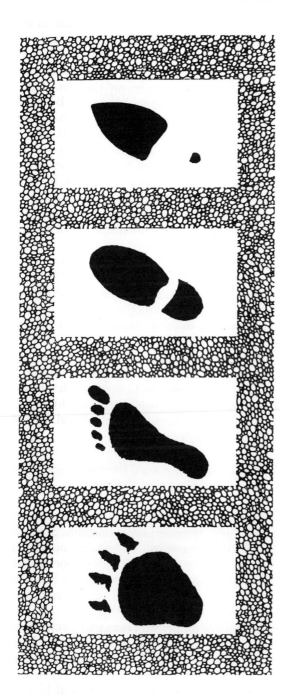

THE EVOLUTION OF AUTHORITY

maintaining but not increasing their position in the 1960s and apparently beginning a new period of advance in the 1980s. Statistically, females formed about 36 per cent of university students in the 1920s and about 25 per cent during the three following decades. These proportions began to increase in the late 1950s, rising to 38 per cent by the late 1970s. Most of the women whom we have interviewed and most of those now available for senior positions, therefore, have acquired their higher education qualifications as part of a cohort in which they were noticeably under-represented.

The post-war years to the 1980s are the period when most of our interviewees have created their careers. In this period, the main tendencies in women's professional development appear to be those of advance, but in very limited fields and often with significant constraints in their personal and their employment lives. In *Who was Who* in 1961 – 70, for instance, the thirty-eight Scotswomen who appeared in the publication had careers primarily in the arts, teaching, medicine and public life. Only half of them had been married, and fewer than a third had had children (Marshall, 1983). As Marshall notes, it was easier to combine marriage with some careers rather than others: the nurses and academics amongst the eminent women were all single.

For most women in the early and middle years of this century in Scotland, then, a choice had to be made between a serious career and marriage. Marshall comments that 'Women with a particular sense of vocation were foregoing marriage, and in areas with formal career structure, it was usually only the single women who achieved eminence.' This finding is reinforced by the fact that, during the post-Second World War years in Scotland, the economic activity of married women was only about two-thirds that of the national average; it began to catch up only in the 1970s and at the end of the 1980s it exceeded the national average (Brown, 1989).

Despite changes in trends, the pattern of present female under-representation in the professional world has characterised the entire period in which women became eligible to enter professional life. In 1977, for instance, Marshall notes that there were still no female directors of education in Scotland and that women professors have been rare indeed. As we write this book at the beginning of the 1990s, this picture has changed only slightly.

Could one explanation be that females' choice of subjects of study has tended to debar them from particularly influential positions? In the early centuries of Scottish education, girls followed a different curriculum from that of boys at school; girls tended to be educated primarily for their future domestic lives as wives and mothers. Even with the coming of comprehensive education, girls and boys continued to follow different subject choices at school and, later, in higher education. In particular, female under-representation in the pure and applied sciences at school and, to an even greater extent, in higher education, has been noted. As Bamford (1988) has shown, most examinable subjects in Scottish schools tend to be highly gendered, with the exception of English and mathematics at O grade. As an illustration of the tendency of subjects to attract primarily men or women in higher education, Mackinlay (1989a) shows that women formed only about 15 per cent of undergraduate entrants to computer science courses in Scottish universities in 1988. In a review of the literature, Sutherland (1990) suggests that women returners to all levels of education seem to opt more for child-care, child psychology, literature and social studies, while men opt more for mathematics and technology.

The unpalatable fact remains, however, that even in those fields in which they predominate — such as secondary school teaching or the arts and social sciences generally — women in Scotland remain almost as under-represented at senior level as they do in professions such as engineering, which are dominated at all levels by men. Subject choice in itself, then, does not appear to be a major factor in the under-representation of women at senior levels.

Do women's levels of attainment in higher education have an adverse effect on their future careers? In particular, many more women than men have studied in the past for ordinary rather than honours degrees at university in Scotland (Marshall, 1983), and far fewer women than men have proceeded to post-graduate qualifications, other than those in teacher training. Evidence from female employment in Britain as a whole also shows that there is a large amount of underachievement in women's early choices of employment as related to their educational attainment (Dex, 1987).

Because we are unaware of any Scottish study which directly investigates the effect of gender on the relationship between educational qualifications and employment patterns, we are unable to give any firm answers to the question about the effect of women's education and training levels on their future occupational levels. It appears that employed women in Scotland themselves believe that 'Women require more qualifications than men to reach the same levels in management' (SIACE, 1990). There is also considerable evidence that, overall, women have not in the past received the same levels of education and training as men in Scotland (Nelson, 1988) or in the United Kingdom as a whole (Byrne, 1978; Acker and Piper, 1984; Wickham, 1986, amongst many others). The combination of requiring a higher standard of qualifications than men but actually receiving a lower standard may well be an important factor in under-representation at senior levels.

As well as education, the role of the Churches has also been highly influential in Scottish life. For many centuries Scotland has been a country where organised religion has played a formative role in shaping civil society. So to what extent might organised religion have played a part in female under-representation in senior posts?

Both of the major religions involved — Protestantism and Catholicism — have a long history of apparently mistrusting women outside a predominantly domestic setting, at times actively attempting to ensure that all major political, economic and social decisions were made by men. Women remain debarred from priesthood in the Roman Catholic Church in Scotland as everywhere else. The formal position of the Catholic Church is to support equal opportunities only as far as possible: 'Women should not assume that they should or could fill exactly the same roles as men, including the ordained ministry' (Petre, 1989). In contrast, by the beginning of the 1990s, a number of the Scottish Protestant Churches, including the Church of Scotland, permit women to act as ministers; the first female minister was ordained in 1970.

We are not aware of any studies which examine in any depth the interaction of religion and the role of women in Scotland. In a study of girls learning Latin and mathematics before 1872, Moore (1984) argues that Presbyterian beliefs have had the effect of restricting girls' access to education and opportunity. She suggests that, while the democratic tradition of Scottish education encourages talented and persevering children to advance, in the Presbyterian tradition it was thought that girls' education should be a preparation for women's role in the home.

More generally, it appears that one effect of organised religion on women's lives in Scotland may have been to deter them from seeking, and men from granting them, any substantial access to senior positions both in the Churches themselves as well as in other forms of employment. The exceptions are, of course, positions at the head of all-female establishments, such as prioresses or abbesses. Thus, Marshall (1983) suggests that 'possibly the only women who sought advancement through their own employment were nuns and mistresses . . . A well-born, able woman could see in a career as an abbess a means of satisfying her ambition.' Female positions of ecclesiastical influence were, of course, characterised by two major features which also mark many secular senior positions occupied by women — the posts themselves were restricted to women, and the women occupying them either had, or tended, to be unmarried.

SOCIAL ATTITUDES
More recently, traditional attitudes towards women in Scotland have begun to change dramatically, at least in the period from the 1970s

onwards. As Burnhill and McPherson (1984) have shown, there have been important shifts in social attitudes, particularly amongst able school leavers — the population from which both senior men and senior women are drawn. They suggest that during the 1970s:

> Major change has occurred both in the configuration of men's and women's expectations about women, and also in the expectations that each woman is likely to have for herself. Qualified women have become more ambitious, educationally and occupationally, and more men and women are now prepated to accept such ambitions as legitimate.

However, the trends depicted by Burnhill and McPherson also indicate how widespread are the social attitudes of both sexes against women trying to fulfil themselves both at home and at work. Even by 1981, amongst able school leavers, nearly 50 per cent of men and 40 per cent of women believed that 'it is rare for a woman to combine a career and a family and make a success of both', while about a third of both men and women agreed that 'men are not keen to marry ''career'' women.'

Restrictive attitudes against women striving for, and achieving, senior positions are held by many women in Scotland, both about their own career expectations and ambitions and about those of their female relatives. Thus, Brown (1990a) has collected from female managers the following sample of adverse comments from older female relatives:

> I don't know why you do it. You don't need the money.

> Why do they keep sending you off on these trips?

> My daughter-in-law [a senior executive] has got herself a 'little job'.

> Well, what do you expect if you have a woman for a solicitor?

> The trouble with you is you want to be loved for your brains, not your face.

> Give it up.

> It has to be you. How could I ask him to give up his job?

Brown comments that 'these remarks are designed to demean ambitious women and to foster their feelings of guilt; they are hurtful and damage the progress which competent women can make.'

Evidence about male attitudes towards women aspiring to, and reaching, senior positions remains scarce in Scotland. Brown (1990a) reports that:

Many men are concerned to try to do what they can about improving the lot of women in senior management. Others, however, particularly those in positions of power, hold entrenched views and do much, consciously or unconsciously, to perpetuate myths about women and to shore up discriminatory practices. A male senior officer in one of the major teachers' unions (with, at the time, a woman president), for instance, stated in public 'the trouble with women is that they are so emotional.'

Burnhill and McPherson (1984) have reported the changes in beliefs about gender roles amongst both male and female able school leavers in Scotland over the period from 1971 to 1981. They show that, between 1971 and 1981, major change has occurred in men's expectations about women. Nevertheless, even in 1981, only 48 per cent of men disagreed with the statement that 'Women can get as much sense of achievement from their husbands' careers as from having a career of their own.' In 1981, only 48 per cent of men disagreed that 'men are not keen to marry "career" women.' Both Burnhill and McPherson, as well as SIACE (1990), show that there are considerable differences between male and female attitudes towards women in careers or management: on all items tested, male attitudes are less positive and more restrictive than female attitudes on women's education, training and employment.

EMPLOYMENT PRACTICES
Once they have completed their education, it appears that many women in Scotland feel restricted by social attitudes in the workplace as well as by the persistence of traditional practices in recruitment, training and promotion. Both in formal research and in 'straw polls' taken on courses for women in management, what respondents refer to as 'men's attitudes' are always top of the list of barriers against women taking up more senior positions. All groups of women employees in banking, insurance, finance and engineering who took part in SIACE group discussions (SIACE, 1990) at Glasgow College reported that:

> Men's attitudes towards women [are] an important hurdle . . . The men whose attitudes are important are customers as well as managers . . . Especially difficult is the 'old school' with traditional ideas . . . Both aspirant groups also felt that male managers underestimate the capabilities of women and therefore restrict their opportunities at work — 'women are inclined to get the lighter side of the jobs, not the complex or more technical aspects.' Manager groups . . . felt that they are perceived by men as a threat and that this could restrict their continuing development.

Earlier in this chapter we noted that there are important differences between male and female attitudes about education, training and employment. There are also, as SIACE (1990) has shown, striking differences between male and female attitudes related to employment practices in the workplace:

> [Male] employers and women employees hold divergent perceptions of issues related to women's management training and development. Employers perceive that, on the whole, there are no hurdles to women's management development, although the need for geographical mobility, international considerations and women's domestic responsibilities can create particular difficulties for women. By contrast, female employees perceive that difficulties in women's management development include men's and women's attitudes to women; organisational factors, such as lack of child care and career breaks; male numerical dominance; conflict between work on the one hand and home and family on the other hand; and women's relative lack of understanding of organisational politics.

SIACE (1990) has also shown that most female employees and (largely male) employers believe that sex discrimination has diminished in their organisation in recent years, but that fewer than half of women employees believe that equal opportunities exist throughout their organisation. Mosson (1990) suggested at a major Scottish conference that the most important step required to improve the representation of women in management in Scotland was to change male attitudes.

Other evidence concerns the extent to which the attitudes of professional women themselves appear to deter them from seeking out more senior positions. In Strathclyde Region, 60 per cent of unpromoted teachers are women, but there is on average only one woman for every sixty-eight male applicants for posts of head-teachers in secondary schools and one in twenty-three for posts of deputy head-teacher. Yet the percentage rates of success amongst these few women in achieving senior positions are higher than for men (Brown, 1990a). It appears, then, that women do not apply for senior posts for which their ability and their experience would qualify them.

Much the same conclusion about women in five European countries (including the United Kingdom) emerges in Sutherland (1985). Citing evidence from university women teachers about why women are under-represented in senior posts at universities, she notes that in one university the proportion of women appointed was equal to — possibly a little greater than — the proportion of women applicants. She goes on to note the importance of the attitudes of women themselves: they tend to doubt their own abilities, she says, and they tend to prefer to stay where they are partly because of their enjoyment of work at lectureship level.

Other possible factors in recruitment and promotion practices include the persistence of informal methods. Brown (1990a) comments on the extent to which 'people rate highly and appoint and promote those who think like them and follow similar philosophies'. She goes on to cite examples from head-teachers' ratings of umpromoted teachers, HMI appointments and membership of national working parties in education where HMI patronage is crucial. Sutherland (1985) refers to the effect of informal appointments procedures as a likely factor in women's under-representation at senior level in universities. In making appointments, the United Kingdom is, she says, the most vague in its statements of what is required and how achievement is assessed; it also has the lowest proportion of female staff in senior university positions amongst the five European countries which she studied.

More broadly, although by no means conclusively, there appears to be some evidence that the equal opportunities (gender) policies which are now in place in about two-thirds of Scottish employers may not yet have had a significant effect on practice (Fitzgerald, 1989; Fowler, 1989; SIACE, 1990). A variety of different factors appear to be implicated in this lack of effectiveness. SIACE (1990) has identified, amongst other possible factors, relative passivity in implementing equal opportunities policies, lack of performance appraisal for non-managerial staff, lack of arrangements to enable women to combine family and work re-sponsibilities, lack of female role models in management and the persistence of an old boys' network amongst male managers. Moreover, as Nelson (1989) shows, women tend to receive significantly less training from their employers than men.

Another factor in employment practice which may disadvantage women from achieving senior positions is age discrimination. Sex discrimination cases considered by industrial tribunals in the United Kingdom have shown that age bars to recruitment to particular university posts have discriminated against women (Jones vs the University of Manchester, 1988; Huppert vs the University Grants Commission and the University of Cambridge, 1986). Although we have not conducted a formal survey, at first glance it appears that substantial numbers of references to age continue to appear in Scottish job advertisements for professional and managerial posts.

Although not documented for Scotland specifically, another factor appears to be the effect of marriage and child rearing on female career patterns. Dex (1987) has shown that, for Britain as a whole, female professionals frequently lost professional status following their husband's move to a different geographical location, while downward occupational mobility was common for all groups following career breaks for child rearing. A major contributing factor in such trends is likely to be the relatively low level of affordable child care in Scotland, where public sector pre-school provision has for many years run at levels even below those in the rest of Britain, which are, in turn, lower than in most of the rest of the European Community (Cohen, 1989).

GENDER INSENSITIVITY

Paterson and Fewell (1990) argue that 'it is because [gender inequality] is so deeply embedded that gender discrimination has not been an issue in Scottish education. Its absence as an issue is not because there is no problem or because any problem is in the process of solving itself, but because until recently its existence as a problem has not been identified.'

Commenting on Scottish educational research, Gerver and Johnston (1990) have concluded that:

> Much Scottish educational research appears to ignore gender . . . Where one might expect to find some mention of gender patterns, there is often a deafening silence . . . One reason is that often the basic information is lacking. Gerver's 1990 survey of ten years of the Manpower Services Commission in Scotland shows that MSC figures for participation in adult training are rarely analysed by sex. [Scottish Education Department statistical] bulletins have until recently been inconsistent in presenting sex-differentiated data. The SED's priorities are not directly concerned with any aspect of gender differences . . . Interpretation of results of educational research in Scotland also often yields less information about gender differences than a neutral observer might have expected . . . The Parent's Survey recently carried out on a national sample for the Scottish Education Department did not analyse results to explore possible gender differences, although sex data were collected. We can think of other instances where gender data were simply unavailable, available but not analysed or available but inconsistently analysed.

As Bamford (1988) shows, where information about gender and education is available and analysed, significant findings emerge:

> Gender differences are accepted and expected by teachers and others both in pre-five and in primary education. At secondary level the research shows significant differences in boys' and girls' subject choice and levels of attainment . . . In teaching, research confirms that despite the fact that women teachers have for many years outnumbered men, women are significantly under-represented in promoted posts . . . Research into adult education in Scotland points to important differences in men's and women's access to education, their choice of courses, their motivation for returning to study and the timing of their learning experiences. Research into further and higher education highlights the different limitations expressed by each sex in subject choice.

Gender issues in employment also appear not to have been generally recognised in Scotland. The main interest in this area in Scotland has lain on tracing the extent to which women working in Scotland tend to be concentrated in low-paid, often (but not always) low-skill jobs (see, for example, Breitenbach, 1989). By contrast, information about women in management in the private sector is, as SIACE notes, 'virtually non-existent.' In the public sector, Brown (1990a) has found that 'reliable and comprehensive facts and figures on women in management . . . were not readily available.'

The issue of gender in employment in senior positions does appear sporadically in the national Scottish press (see, for example, Nelson, 1988; Robertson, 1989; Muir, 1989). Because of the lack of any more extensive research investigations into the field, however, the evidence cited tends to be purely statistical — so many (or, rather, so few) women lawyers, female appointments to public bodies and so on. Very recently, with the development of women's or equal opportunities committees and officers in local authorities, central government and elsewhere, there has been an increasing number of analyses of gender in employment at different levels in individual organisations; a few such studies have been noted in the previous section of this chapter.

Does this apparent lack of awareness of gender both in education and in employment mean that it may in itself be a factor in the particularly low levels of female representation in senior positions in Scotland? The evidence from experience in other countries suggest that, indeed, it may be. In the United States, for instance, levels of awareness of gender imbalance are widespread, and levels of female representation are much higher than in Scotland. In Denmark, on the other hand, levels of awareness of gender as an issue in education are about as low as they are in Scotland and women are roughly as under-represented in senior positions in education as they are in Scotland (Commission of the European Communities, 1989).

Any precise casual link between lack of gender awareness and low levels of female representation at senior level is, of course, impossible to prove. But it is at least likely that lack of gender awareness inhibits employers from investigating seriously their own policies and procedures for recruitment, training and promotion; as a result, those practices which deter women from reaching senior positions may continue unchecked. Moreover, as we have already suggested, the lack of such awareness means that insufficient data about male and female patterns of education, training, and employment are available. Policy-makers are thus unable to assess the precise dimensions of the problem or to try to plan strategically to address it in the future.

Conclusion

As we have suggested, there appears to be a relative lack of data and analysis about women in senior positions in both the private and the public sector in Scotland. What data are available suggest that women, where they are present at all at senior levels, probably form no more than about 5 per cent of the occupants of such posts. The fact of such under-representation has, however, not generally been recognised as an issue in Scotland. Although there is no necessary connection between the numbers of women represented at senior level and organisations' awareness of gender as an issue, it may well be that the very low levels of female representation in political life in Scotland are one factor in the apparent lack of interest in such issues.

In trying to investigate these and other factors in this book through the eyes of fifty women interviewees, we are, of course, looking at highly selective evidence. The views of our survivors are likely to be very different from those who aspired and failed, those who chose domestic over public life, and those who have never even hoped for any power in their communities. Even our survivors, however, tend to believe that Scotland offers a predominantly hostile climate for women seeking senior positions. In support of this assessment, they refer particularly to the paucity of senior women, male chauvinism and women's low expectations of themselves.

Historical evidence suggests that women in Scotland have been characterised by hard work, humour and determination. However, their experience has been marked by significant constraints in both their personal and their employment lives. Until recently, they have been noticeably under-represented in entry to higher education, and they have tended to choose different fields of study from men. Despite evidence that they may require higher levels of qualification than men to reach the same levels of seniority, women, at least until recently, have tended to achieve lower levels in higher education and to receive less training from their employers.

Another important factor in female under-representation at senior levels appears to be the persistence of the traditional attitude that women's place is in the home. Since the 1970s, attitudes towards women in Scotland have begun to change dramatically, with able school leavers increasingly accepting the legitimacy of strengthened female ambitions. But important differences between male and female attitudes towards women's ambitions persist, with male attitudes consistently less positive and more restrictive.

Other factors in the under-representation of women in senior positions appear to include the persistence of traditional practices in recruitment, training and promotion, women's reluctance to apply for senior posts, and what many commentators refer to as 'male attitudes' in the workplace. It appears that, so far at least, equal opportunities policies have not had a major effect on levels of female representation at senior levels. Factors which appear to be implicated in this ineffectiveness include employers' relative passivity in implementing equal opportunities, the lack of performance appraisal for non managerial staff, the lack of arrangements for women to combine work and family, the lack of female role models in management, the persistence of an 'old boys'' network, and age discrimination. For many women, it appears as if both marriage and child care result in downward occupational mobility, both because of the effect of husbands' relocation and because of the lack of good quality, affordable child care. An additional factor in female under representation may be the relative lack of gender sensitivity in research into education and employment in Scotland.

Nevertheless, the picture which we have painted largely reflects the past. At the beginning of 1990s, it appears that the numbers of females in senior posts are increasing; indeed, even during the months of writing this book, we have had to revise the designations of a number of our interviewees as they move into even more senior posts. It also appears as if gender itself is increasingly becoming an issue in research, in education, in the professions and in management. For instance, explicit attention has been paid to gender in the composition of the board of Scottish Enterprise and the boards of some of the Local Enterprise Companies. Scottish Enterprise is also requiring LEC boards to take account of equal opportunities, including gender, in their business plans. The launch in 1990 of Training 2000: the Scottish Alliance for Women's Training, an organisation which aims to improve the quality and quantity of women's training in Scotland, also augurs well for the future. Meanwhile, an increasing number of publications deal with gender issues in Scotland (see, for example, Burnhill and McPherson, 1984; Bamford, 1988; McKinlay, 1989; Scott, 1989; Brown and Fairley, 1990; Gerver and Johnston, 1990; Paterson and Fewell, 1990). At the beginning of the 1990s, then, it appears as if much of what we have written in this chapter may have to be substantially revised within a few years.

Meanwhile, what do our interviewees have to say about their backgrounds, their educational experiences, their career patterns, their working practices, their domestic lives, and the prospects for the future? We hope that their reports and the analysis of their experience will help towards understanding the recent past, and current experience, of women in Scotland. In particular we hope that their accounts will become part of a growing recognition of the highly significant impact of gender on domestic and public life. Our interviewees have experienced, and reflected seriously on, work and achievement in Scotland today. It is to their first hand accounts that we shall now turn.

Chapter Two

The Cradle of Ambition

Introduction

As children and young women, our interviewees tended to lead outwardly conventional, often privileged lives. Their generally stable family backgrounds appear to have led to successful academic achievement at school followed by direct entry to higher education, the award of a degree and, often, subsequent professional training. But how far is such a general impression really true? And, even if the details do confirm the general picture, why do so few other women with similar backgrounds achieve to the same extent as our interviewees, when many more of their brothers occupy senior positions? Are there any specific factors in the early lives of our fifty women which seem to have contributed to their later achievements? After summarising the main patterns below, this chapter will explore these questions in an analysis of the families and the initial education experiences of the fifty women interviewed.

The overwhelming impression given by our interviewees is that their family backgrounds were fundamentally stable and secure. Against this stable background, however, disturbing factors sometimes appeared, such as the early death or prolonged illness of a parent, or frequent and often painful relocations. Most were brought up in urban or semi-urban communities in Scotland, although over a quarter were brought up in England or abroad.

Two thirds of the interviewees' fathers worked at professional or managerial level, and nearly one third held skilled or semi-skilled manual jobs; there were a few cross-class households. Under half of the mothers stayed at home, with the rest working full-time or part-time, often only when their children were older. Most interviewees identified closely with one parent, who was as often their mother as their father. Many mothers were seen as strong and influential both within their families and often in their communities as well. Most of the parents were ambitious for their children to be well educated.

About two-thirds of the interviewees were only children or the eldest in their family. Most reported that they had felt that they were different from many of their friends: many remembered being tomboys; several were openly rebellious; many grew up introverted and spent a great deal of time reading; many felt that they were pursuing interests or paths not shared by others around them. A few felt that, at least outwardly, they had been reasonably conventional as children.

Their interests at home and at school included the arts as well as individual and team sport. In most households, either political or religious affiliation played an important role, with Protestantism and socialism prevalent.

Most of the interviewees attended local primary schools and selective secondary schools, with a relatively high proportion attending single sex schools. Nearly two-thirds attended state schools, with over a third attending fee paying schools. They mainly enjoyed school and did well academically.

After finishing school, three-quarters of the girls continued directly to university or other forms of higher education. Nearly all of those from middle-class backgrounds did so, primarily because it was assumed that they would, rather than because they had any particular career directions in view. The patterns for those from working-class backgrounds were more varied. Just over half of these whose fathers were manual workers entered paid employment immediately after finishing school; although a number of them would have preferred to continue to higher education, their families discouraged such aspirations either for financial or for social reasons. Nevertheless, a substantial number of the young women from working-class backgrounds proceeded directly to further or higher education, while nearly all the rest entered higher education as mature students.

At university the interviewees studied primarily the arts and social sciences, almost equally divided between ordinary and honours first degrees. Although only a relatively small number continued immediately on to further study, many later acquired postgraduate and professional qualifications. Despite the widespread lack of guidance in choosing their courses, most enjoyed their time at university; a number, however, felt that they had underachieved in a way characteristic of many young women of their generation.

Of those who did not continue their education after they completed school, about half became clerical workers, with the rest spread amongst a variety of occupations, including journalism, the armed services, a family business and hotel work. Of those who graduated from university, the largest number trained as teachers or immediately began to teach or to lecture. Many others continued with academic study or professional training. The first destinations of the rest included working in a library, a trade union, research, engineering, computing, hotel management, interpretation, marketing and entering the family business. As we shall see later, however, in most cases such first destinations bore little resemblance to future careers.

Girls at home

PARENTS AND SIBLINGS
Most of our interviewees were children and adolescents during the middle years of the century. Their age distribution is as follows:

Figure 12

AGE DISTRIBUTION OF INTERVIEWEES

age range	%
20 – 29	4
30 – 39	36
40 – 49	38
50 – 59	12
60 +	10

No. of Interviewees = 50

According to the father's occupation, about two-thirds of families (68 per cent) would be generally regarded as belonging to the middle classes, with just under one-third (30 per cent) being placed in the working classes; it was impossible to place one interviewee in such a classification. Almost all of the fathers worked full-time (94 per cent); one was unemployed and two died early in the interviewees' childhood. During interviewees' adolescence, as many mothers worked as stayed at home full-time, as the following table shows:

Figure 13

EMPLOYMENT STATUS OF MOTHERS

	%
Full-Time at Home	44
Part-Time Employment	24
Full-Time Employment	20
Ill	4
Dead	2
Not Known	6

No. of Interviewees = 50

The level of parental education was reasonably high: of those for whom we obtained information about parental education, 46 per cent of fathers and 35 per cent of mothers held higher education qualifications.

Most characteristically, our interviewees were only or eldest children in their families:

Figure 14

POSITION IN FAMILY

	%
Eldest Child	18
Only Child	48
Younger/Youngest Child	26
Middle Child	4

No. of Interviewees = 50

Of those from middle-class families, most siblings have subsequently pursued professional careers. Of those from working-class backgrounds, most siblings, unlike their sister interviewees, are employed in skilled, highly gendered manual occupations such as hairdressing or firefighting.

Nearly three-quarters of interviewees' families lived in Scotland throughout their childhood and adolescence; of the remaining thirteen, eleven lived primarily in England (although with postings abroad in several cases), while two lived primarily in North America.

HAPPY FAMILIES?

If Tolstoy in *Anna Karenina* had been right about the similarity of all happy families, the stable, secure backgrounds reported by most of our interviewees would offer little analytical interest. We heard many variants on the recollection of 'a happy but firm childhood'. The words, 'sheltered', 'protected', 'stable', 'secure', 'comfortable', 'loving', and 'settled' recur frequently:

I had a happy childhood, with a pleasant, supportive upbringing.

Both my parents were very loving towards me.

My upbringing was secure in a firm but happy home.

My background was very straight and conventional — extremely stable.

I had a privileged, comfortable upbringing.

I had a normal, happy childhood, leading a sheltered life.

There were, however, a number of indications that the gift of security as children resulted from a deliberate effort by parents rather than stemming automatically from a close parental relationship, a geographically stable environment or a comfortable income.

> I had a good relationship with both my parents, although I'm not sure how close they were to each other. My childhood gave me a sense of security and a confident base.'

> I now wonder how my mother managed the amount of housework that had to be done. She must have been a wizard with money, to keep the whole family well dressed, well fed and well cared for. But my father was more dominant than my mother. He had a drink problem, and there were many arguments.'

> When I was a child our family moved often; by the time I was twelve, I had lived in seven different places on two continents. But, despite so much moving around, I remember a mainly stable, secure family life. Loyalty to each other was, as it still is, fundamental. I have always felt that, regardless of the circumstances and wherever they are, I could go home for help from my family.'

In striking contrast to the prevailing theme of fundamental stability during childhood, a few interviewees report recollections of major disruption or turbulence in their families. Most typically, problems related to fathers' drinking:

> The relationship between my parents was stable until I was in my teens. Then my father started to drink because of pressures at work. I was told by [my family] that I couldn't even consider moving away from home to go to university — that I would have to stay because I was the youngest, and I was the only female — the only one who could be a support to my mother.

Interviewees occasionally mention domestic friction and its aftermath:

> I remember that when I was a teenager there were many rows at home — my parents' marriage was far from strong.

> While I was at university my parents divorced. This made me aware of the importance of having a secure financial base for myself, because my mother was left poorly off.

In a few cases, the illness or death of a parent during an interviewee's childhood contributed to difficulties as children. Sometimes, however, such personal circumstances appear to have developed qualities which interviewees believe to have been important in their later life:

> My mother died when I was eighteen months old and I was looked after by my female relatives. I lacked a sense of security.

> My father died when I was thirteen, and my mother returned to clerical work. I had a more serious upbringing because of his death — there was less money for frills.

> Because of my mother's illness, I was brought up mainly by my father, my uncle and my grandfather. As a result I became close to men and have always been comfortable in male environments. My father, who was very involved in the trade union movement, used to take me to union meetings in the evening.

Nevertheless, the prevalent picture is one of stable lives as children. Within this general pattern, daughters' perceptions of their interactions with parents tend to fall into several clusters of characteristics rather than demonstrating any one clear trend. Parental expectations, the dominance of one parent or the other, and religious and political allegiances appear to have been particularly important in shaping their daughters' self images as children and adolescents.

PARENTAL EXPECTATIONS

Parental expectations of their daughters — their ambitions and their requirements — tended to fall into three main types. Of these clusters, by far the largest consists of parents who were ambitious for their daughters, because of what they saw as the crucial importance of education as preparation for the world of work. Characteristic comments include:

> My mother was extremely ambitious for both her children.

> Both my parents were very keen that both daughters should be well educated.

> Books were always important in our family. My mother, who was more highly educated, was more obviously influential, but my father also had high expectations of his children.

In many such homes, the pattern typically was that both boys and girls were expected to contribute equally to domestic duties:

> All of us had to help out when I was young; it was a good training for us. There was no difference between my upbringing and that of my brothers.

But parents were not always consistent in their academic and their domestic expectations, as we can see from a second cluster of attitudes.

One interviewee, whose parents expected equal academic achievement from all their children, comments:

> My mother simply assumed that my sister and I would take a full part of all the domestic responsibilities. My brothers helped only occasionally.

Another had also experienced an early version of the double role:

> When I was thirteen my mother had cancer, so I had a lot of extra responsibilities from then until I was nineteen, when she died. I did a lot of housework and nearly all the chores. It was simply expected, without discussion, that I could cope with them and study for my qualifications at school.

In a third cluster of attitudes, gender appears to have shaped a substantial number of parents' ambitions for their children, as the following comments suggest:

> There were some differences between my own and my brother's upbringing — there was less emphasis on my own education.

> My father was always very ambitious for his son, but, unfortunately, according to my father, it was the daughter who had got the brains, not the son.

> My parents simply assumed that both my sisters and I would go on to university and would qualify for professional work. But they also believed that our future employment would not be significant in itself; instead, it would be an insurance in case we became spinsters or widows — the possibility that we might become divorcees was not mentioned. My father held strongly that, as he put it, 'it's a man's job to bring home the bacon and the woman's job is to cook it.'

Despite the gender-restricted expectations of some parents, however, the great majority of interviewees went immediately from school to higher education, as we shall discuss further in the next part of this chapter. We heard no reports of choices being made to educate brothers in preference to their sisters, either at school level or in further or higher education. The variety of attitudes thus appears, unexpectedly, to have resulted in largely uniform practice.

PARENTAL DOMINANCE

Most interviewees report that one parent had been dominant in their family, but such influence was as likely to be held by mothers as by fathers. Nor did whether mothers worked appear to be related to whether they were perceived as dominant. A number of interviewees comment, however, that their mothers should have worked but did not — a reflection of the prevailing mid-century social climate in which mothers were more often expected to chair voluntary groups than to sit in board rooms.

Despite the diversity of patterns, one trend does stand out: interviewees were much more likely to identify with the parental figure whom they perceived to be in charge, regardless of sex. The characteristics praised in both fathers and mothers tend to be ones linked to achievement in the wider world rather than predominantly to domestic values: impressive organising skills, hard work, intelligence, and challenging the status quo are all qualities which our interviewees admired in their parents and which appear to have been important in their own adult lives. The following are a representative sample of such comments.

> My mother was the most dominant influence on me. A local councillor, she was outspoken on many issues.

> I very much respected my mother. She was the dominant one in our house. She was always very organised, and helped in the business as well as running our home.

> My mother was a strongly principled person who always questioned anything she didn't like. She has been a very strong influence on me. As well as working full-time, she used to be involved in the local woman's guild in the church — until the minister preached that women should be at home and not work. At that stage my mother walked out of the church.

> I was always conscious of being closer to my father than my mother; I admired enormously his hard work, relentless questioning of accepted orthodoxies, and community service. But I also resented the amount of time that his other commitments took away from spending with us children.

> I was very like my father and was always very close to him. I admired him very much. My hard work — when I am hard working — I get from my father. I saw him as a role model. I can see now in my mother a lot of traits which I do admire: she is intelligent, extremely witty, and very strong minded. But I was not close to her as a child.

> My father was much more intelligent than my mother and he encouraged me to learn. I was much closer to him than to my mother.

YOUTHFUL ALLEGIANCES
As well as being shaped by the characteristics of parents with whom they identified, interviewees' sense of themselves was also bound up with the

religious and political allegiances of their households. Nearly three-quarters of our interviewees report that, as children, they were strongly committed either to politics or religion or both.

Figure 15

ALLEGIANCES

	%
Religion Important	46
Politics Important	41
No Allegiances	28

No. of Interviewees = 46

Religion played an important role in 46 per cent of interviewees' families. Overall, the religious affiliation of families was predominantly Protestant or of mixed faith (86 per cent), with 14 per cent being brought up in Roman Catholic homes; no other religious affiliation is mentioned by the interviewees. A much higher proportion of interviewees from Roman Catholic homes report that religion had been influential when they were growing up and, indeed, remained important during their adult life. For both faiths — particularly for those brought up in households of mixed faith — interviewees' dominant emphasis lay on living out religious values and ethics:

> I was brought up to be caring of other people and aware of their needs because of my Catholic upbringing. Many nuns were role models for me.

> Religion was important in my childhood and it still is. It has given me exacting standards and a value system. The reality of the Church is much harsher than just believing in the gospels.

> I think I've been very lucky in life, and I lead in many ways a very selfish life. Once a week attending church to think about things other than myself is not a great deal to expect.

In a few cases, religious observance as well as the Christian ethical system mattered deeply to interviewees:

> Religion has always been very important to me — always very enriching in my life.

> I was brought up in a household strongly imbued with religion, and the Church of Scotland is still important to me; I am an elder in the church.

Particularly striking are the numbers of interviewees who comment on their having learned political as well as social values through their religious commitment:

> My strong Catholic upbringing left me with a sense of values which I have never forgotten, particularly of social justice and anti-racism.

> I was brought up to believe in the Christian value system. I still believe in justice and equality.

In several cases, however, religious teachings were perceived to be at odds with the idea of sexual equality, and interviewees found themselves rejecting their former beliefs on those grounds:

> My family were not church oriented, but I liked the Church of England and was confirmed as a teenager. For a while in my adult life, religion continued to be important, but I later lost my faith, mainly because of the Church's attitudes towards women.

Although only six interviewees say that both religion and politics had been important to them as children, comments such as these imply an important cross-over between religious and political commitment and values. It is thus not surprising to find that politics was reported as important in their childhood by 41 per cent of our interviewees.

In twelve of the eighteen households in which it mattered and for which political affinity was mentioned, politics meant socialism. Commitment to socialism was felt strongly in both working- and middle-class homes: six working-class and six middle-class families were strongly committed at least to socialist values if not actually to the Labour Party. Two interviewees report commitment to the Scottish National Party, and two others to the Conservative Party. While the level of political awareness was high, however, party allegiances were by no means consistent within families. One interviewee commented that her father was a Tory, her mother and elder brother Liberal, her other brother a socialist, while she was committed to Scottish nationalism. And our figures do not include the response from one interviewee that her mother was a closet Conservative while her father was an armchair socialist.

The level of personal identification with political affiliation was generally high. Thus:

> When I was at boarding school my pinups were always well known female politicians. At one stage I fancied myself as the first female Prime Minister!

In another case, an interviewee chose to study Scottish history at university primarily because of her commitment to Scottish nationalism.

A third interviewee selected a doctoral dissertation topic that allowed her to explore her personal interest in the tension between revolutionary and conservative political ideology and practice.

So far, then, the picture emerging of our interviewees is that of girls who, growing up in fundamentally stable homes, tended to identify with the dominant parent and to internalise their families' religious and political commitments. Although diverse, their parents' expectations typically resulted in their daughters' proceeding to higher education in far higher numbers even than their relatively well-educated parents.

But what of their personal qualities? How do they now recall their main characteristics as children and adolescents? Here again, it is notable that the characteristics on which interviewees dwelt tend to be those likely to correlate with later achievement, particularly independence, organisational skills and sheer hard work.

INDEPENDENT SPIRITS

Perhaps the most significant theme running through our interviewees' accounts of childhood is that of independence. Characteristically, parents actively encouraged their daughter's independence, particularly fostering her ability to make decisions:

> My parents always encouraged me to make choices, to make decisions by myself. They would present choices to me and then leave me to make up my own mind about them. I chose to go to a fee-paying single-sex school. It was only in later life that I realised what personal sacrifices my parents had made to send me there.

> I had a fairly traditional, conformist upbringing. But my parents always gave me a lot of choice about what I should do, especially as far as social conscience was concerned. One year I moved to an all-black high school by my own choice, although I left after one year. Even as a child I was very conscious of the large amount of independence which my parents encouraged.

> My younger brother and I led very independent lives. When we were twelve and thirteen, we announced that we didn't want anyone to look after us after school, that we were quite capable of doing things for ourselves. From that time onwards, we cleaned our own rooms, did our own shopping, organised our lunch, and looked after ourselves after school.

In some cases — particularly for those who were only children — independence involved having, or choosing, to be fairly solitary:

> I was a great reader and spent a lot of time on my own — I was quite a solitary child.

I was conscious of being an only child and was quite lonely.

I was quite introverted as a child, and I read a great deal. Indeed, I used to wonder how people could ever get to know anything from contact with other people — most of my understanding of other people, such as it was, came from books.

I was happy on my own. You did tend to live in your own imagination in the 1950s. There was no television, no video. I enjoyed fairly solitary activities such as art and sewing.

Even of those who report frequent contact with other children, there was typically a sense of being odd or different:

I had lots of friends when I was young, but I always felt quite different — the odd one out.

I was singled out at an early age at school as being clever — a halo effect which made me feel quite lonely as a child. I liked solitary pursuits — reading, writing poetry, sewing, knitting.

When I was young I saw myself as being slightly unconventional and something special — slightly different from, and better than, the other girls in my class.

Independence also showed itself in our interviewees' unconventionality as children:

I was quite a wild and unconventional girl — outgoing and gregarious.

I was unconventional in some ways when I was young. I didn't play with dolls, and I was very keen to be as good as the boys.

A substantial number refer explicitly to having been tomboys:

I was a tomboy when I was young and happy on my own.

I was a bit of a tomboy and a loner when I was young. My main hobbies were reading and cycling.

I was a bit of a tomboy — the son my father never had.

One interviewee makes explicit the connection between her androgynous experiences as an adolescent tomboy and her later preference for working with both sexes:

When I was a teenager, a group of us — both girls and boys — used to play together constantly. We skied, played rounders, skated, played cops and robbers, swam, and — best of all — played football. Ever since, I have preferred to work together in teams of both men and women.

Interviewees also place considerable emphasis on their questioning attitudes as children:

I was outgoing, gregarious and reasonably conventional as a child, although I liked to think of myself as being quite unconventional — I always questioned matters both at home and at school.

I was a practical and inquisitive child who always wanted to find out how things worked. My inquisitiveness has stayed with me through my life.

I was a fairly conformist child who generally sought approval from authorities. But I had my own views, which were different from many of those around me. I preferred classical music to pop, and was not a follower of fashion in clothes.

By contrast, a minority of interviewees recall conforming childhoods:

I was a conforming child who liked structures.

I was a perfectionist, introvert and conformist as a child.

Looking back, I can see that I was desperately conventional and probably a bit snobbish.

But, in one instance, parental compulsion to conform where the interviewee preferred independence, resulted in an explosive rejection of conventional expectations:

Both my parents were very strict discipliniarians. They were strong socialists, and religion was extremely important. So my upbringing was very different from that of other young girls in the neighbourhood. I was seen by my school as a difficult, rebellious child and left abruptly in the middle of fourth year, much to my parents' and the school's concern.'

BORN ORGANISERS?
As well as being predominantly independent as children, most interviewees see themselves as having been born organisers — the word 'bossy' occurred frequently — and describe things they had organised as children:

When I was young I had a reputation of being extremely bossy. I loved organising things at home and at school. Once I organised all the neighbourhood children into putting on a play and gymnastic display to raise money for a local home for the blind. After weeks of preparation, followed by the actual performance itself, I went to deliver the money we had raised to the headmistress of the school. I shall never forget the sense of overwhelming pleasure that I had organised something which had resulted in a tangible benefit.

Although I was an introvert, I was always an organiser — a sensible child. I also thought vaguely of being a teacher. However, this idea was suggested to me only because I liked nothing better than to have all my friends sitting round about while I pretended to be a teacher with a blackboard. Looking back, this showed my bossy, organising streak rather than a basic ability in teaching.

I've always been very close to my mother, and helped quite a bit to bring up my brother and sister. If you had talked to them they would have called me quite a bossy big sister.

I was always the one in charge — a strategic minx.

I always liked organising things. At school I used to help with the supervision of younger classes.

The assumption of responsibility was not always freely chosen, however. In a substantial number of cases, our interviewees reported the hard work for which they were responsible because of family circumstances or parental pressure:

As the eldest in a large family, I had a lot of responsibilities. I was used to being in charge, doing the dirty jobs, coping with crisis. I saw myself more as a sister than a daughter to my mother.

Although an only child, I was not spoiled — I had many household chores.

Because my mother worked in a local hospital, my sister and I had a lot of domestic chores.

Overall, then, our interviewees recall a childhood of fundamental stability, in which parents encouraged them to academic achievement and to think and act for themselves. Within this environment, most interviewees identified with the parent whom they perceived as being in charge and showed a marked preference for organising people both within and outwith their family. But what happened when these characteristics encountered the formal education system? Did our interviewees make largely conventional or unconventional choices at school? And what did they decide to do — and why — once they completed school? These questions form the basis of the two following sections of this chapter.

Girls at school

ACADEMIC ACHIEVEMENT

To a very much greater extent than their contemporaries, our fifty interviewees succeeded extraordinarily well at school. A large majority of them achieved qualifications enabling them to enter higher education. A small minority left school with no qualifications, while one achieved a few O levels.

Figure 16

SCHOOL LEAVING QUALIFICATIONS

	%
Highers/A Levels	82
O Levels	2
No Qualifications	16

No. of Interviewees = 50

To some extent, this level of academic achievement correlates, as one would expect, with the level of parental education. For instance, all of those interviewees whose parents were graduates qualified for entry to higher education. We were also not surprised to find that, of those who left school without any qualifications and began paid employment, three-quarters were from working class backgrounds, where parents themselves had no direct experience of higher education. Rather more interesting, however, is the disproportionate number of girls, from families with no experience of higher education themselves, who nevertheless qualified for entry to it. Over half of those who qualified for higher education came from families in which they were the first generation to do so. Such an achievement is out of all proportion to the increases in participation in higher education between the earlier and the middle decades of the century, although it does, of course, reflect increased access to higher education in the UK from the 1960s onwards.

The subjects in which our interviewees' qualifications were obtained followed characteristically different patterns for those in Scotland and in England, as we had expected. In Scotland, even those who described themselves as 'very arts oriented' almost invariably combined at least one science with a grouping of arts subjects; a particularly characteristic pattern was English, French, history, science and maths. By contrast, amongst those at schools in England, the A level system resulted in a characteristic pattern of English, history and French, or physics, chemistry and maths.

Scottish interviewees thus had a much wider range of academic options available to them as they left school. As we shall see in more detail later, however, both English and Scottish girls chose the arts, sciences, social sciences or various professional courses in roughly similar numbers: indeed, the proportion of those choosing arts undergraduate courses was exactly 40 per cent for both the English and the Scots. The wider options available to Scottish pupils are thus not reflected in their actual choices of higher education.

As we have noted earlier in this chapter, interviewees' families generally encouraged their daughters to do well at school, in conformance with the traditional Scottish belief in the value of education both for its own sake and for its vocational advantages. Many of our interviewees, however, were unlike their contemporaries in the kind of schools which they attended. Because of the changes in the Scottish and English school systems over the decades during which our interviewees grew up, it is not feasible to analyse differences in the numbers attending selective or comprehensive schools. But it is striking that, in the period before all Scottish state schools became comprehensive, all but two of those who attended state schools were in senior rather than junior secondaries.

Another difference from their contemporaries lies in the extent to which our interviewees went to fee paying schools. As compared with about only 6 per cent of Scottish pupils as a whole, about one third (34 per cent) attended such schools. In several cases, they held scholarships or bursaries, but a number of parents with low incomes made considerable sacrifices to pay fees for schools with especially high academic reputations. The fact that rather more pupils in England than in Scotland attend fee paying schools was not reflected amongst interviewees: girls brought up primarily in England formed 22 per cent of our interviewees, and 24 per cent of those attending non-state schools.

ATTITUDES TOWARDS SCHOOL

On the whole, the high level of academic achievement by most of our interviewees was accompanied by enjoyment of school and, often, the adoption of one or more teachers as a role model. A characteristic comment was:

> I enjoyed school. My French teacher was especially influential and became a role model for me.

But a liking for school also characterised those who left without qualifications. All but two of this group said that they liked school and, indeed, had done well at it. As we shall see later, most of them left school because of social or economic pressures, rather than because they did not

Cartoon by Jacky Fleming.

succeed academically. Conversely, a number of those who acquired Highers or A levels said that they had hated school.

Of those who stayed on to qualify, several felt they had hardly to work at all to achieve academically:

> My time at school was largely happy. I was naturally bright but also naturally lazy. I was definitely not a grafter at school. I found arts subjects easier than science and therefore studied them. But in some ways I was disappointed in school — definitely by some of the teachers. I wasn't taught skills for living, which should be part of everyone's education.

> In my last years at school I had the definite advantage that, because of many changes of school in the past, I had already covered much of the syllabus. So I made a kind of fetish out of never being seen actually to work, until immediately before the final examinations.

> I was academic and enjoyed school. I put in little effort to do well.

With a very few exceptions, there were scarcely any references to school as challenging or exciting. Rather, their school experience seems to have been for our interviewees merely an inevitable stage in their lives, normally a stepping stone to higher education, but rarely a source of ambition or vocational commitment. Indeed, as we shall see later, a substantial number appeared almost to have drifted into higher education and career choices.

SINGLE SEX SCHOOLING

But what of the experience of those who followed different patterns? Given the broad Scottish tradition of co-education, we were surprised to learn that over a third of our interviewees (38 per cent) had attended single sex schools for at least part of their school life (although one of these single sex schools was a boys' school!). To some extent, of course, this apparent anomaly is accounted for by the fact that a relatively high proportion (34 per cent) attended fee-paying schools, many of which were single sex.

What effect did such a choice have in their lives? There appears to have been little in their subsequent academic and career progress that might relate back specifically to their experience of single sex education. On the whole, their choices in higher education covered as narrow a range of subjects as did the choices of those who had attended co-educational schools. Indeed, their sole evident academic difference from those who attended co-educational schools is that all of those who attended single sex schools acquired higher education entrance qualifications, while only 71 per cent of those attending co-educational schools did so. Any more detailed analysis of the possible effect of single sex education amongst our interviewees is, however, confounded by the fact that most single sex schools were both selective and fee paying. Both all those who attended selective schools and all those who attended fee paying ones achieved higher education matriculation.

Nevertheless, a number of interviewees believed that attending single sex schools had an important effect on their academic achievement as well as their social lives both at school and afterwards:

> I was educated throughout at single sex boarding schools, where I found useful role models — there were many powerful women there. There was also a high degree of academic rigour, which I enjoyed.

> I think single sex schooling has a lot of advantages, not the least of them being the fact that there are far fewer distractions. (Two interviewees)

> I transferred to an all-boys' school to do the A levels which I wanted in Latin, Greek and ancient history. In some ways it was a great relief to change from the single sex grammar school which I had been at. I liked the boys' school in many ways and enjoyed my years there. I was, however, looked at as 'that odd girl', being the only female in an all-male environment.'

I found the transition to co-education at university fairly traumatic — boys seemed an intrusion.

LIFE OUTSIDE SCHOOL

Regardless of the type of school which they attended, our fifty interviewees did a great deal more than merely study. Their activities as girls and adolescents were characterised by variety and achievement. Amongst those who mentioned posts of responsibility which they had held at school, there were four head girls, two deputy head girls, four prefects, a school librarian, and a president of the literary and drama society.

Contrary to the general assumption that potential leaders have usually learned appropriate skills and attitudes through sport at school, only about one-third reported that they were sporty at school. Of those who did participate in sports, many took part in a wide range of different sports, both team and individual. Overall, the standard achieved through competition in sport seems to have been very high — references were made to being of county standard, and there were three hockey captains and one netball captain.

Most characteristically, our interviewees took part enthusiastically in a wide range of activities, of which sport was only one. The emphasis was often on performance — most notably in debating and music. Intellectual interests tended to predominate both in and out of school time; most read frequently and widely; a number edited their school publications; and several were politically active. Early interests in questions of feminism were also mentioned as absorbing free time.

But let them speak for themselves:

> When I was young, reading was one of my main interests — for pleasure as well as for self-education. I also enjoyed all outdoor sports and youth hostelling. And I was interested in the history of architecture, especially church architecture. I was also politically conscious from a young age. I've always been interested in the woman's perspective, and from the age of fifteen I joined an organisation called 'Women for Westminster'.

> I enjoyed sports, camping, skiing, walking. I edited the school newspaper and was active in a church group for social reasons.

> When I was at school I used to do all kinds of things: I edited the school magazine, debated, played both team and individual sports (all quite enthusiastically and badly), acted in plays, and took part in student politics. I also read a great deal of literature and philosophy.

> I was good at sports and joined everything.

Life after school

After they left school, nearly three-quarters of our interviewees went directly on to higher education, most often at university. A few entered further education, while others went directly into paid employment.

Figure 17

FIRST DESTINATION AFTER SCHOOL

	%
Higher Education	74
Further Education	6
Paid Employment	20

No. of Interviewees = 50

Here, perhaps above all, there were striking differences in experience between those from middle-class and those from working-class backgrounds:

Figure 18

FIRST DESTINATIONS AFTER SCHOOL

Middle - Class Backgrounds *	
	%
Higher Education	88
Further Education	6
Paid Employment	6
Working - Class Backgrounds * *	
	%
Higher Education	47
Further Education	6
Paid Employment	47

* No. of Interviewees = 34   * * No. of Interviewees = 15

CHOOSING HIGHER EDUCATION

In their late teens, those interviewees who chose to enter higher education did so for a variety of reasons, but vocational commitment was rarely one. Most typically, they simply assumed that, if they passed their examinations with sufficiently good grades, they would go to university or some other form of higher education. Of the three who went on to further non advanced education, none was qualified to enter higher education; because their numbers were so small, they have been omitted from the following analysis.

Most interviewees chose their universities and courses with little or no careers guidance, and most decisions were made primarily on the grounds of the subjects that they were best at in school:

> I applied to university to read English because it was my best subject. I now regret this slightly, when I see the breadth of other subjects which I could have studied.

> When I left school I went to university to read physics, which had been my best subject. I think I was motivated both by the possibilities of doing something for the world and by the potential for personal glory as a scientist! But I remember that, as an undergraduate, when I had to write an 'intellectual autobiography' to apply for a fellowship, I found it very difficult to give any plausible reasons why I had chosen physics.

Despite their lack of criteria for choosing as they did, only a few bowed to parental or school pressure to make certain choices. Most made up their own minds, often after considering wildly disparate options:

> There was no careers guidance at school. No one mentioned law or business studies to me. I thought vaguely of being an air hostess and vaguely of studying languages. Eventually I chose a BA in secretarial studies.

> When I left school I had no real idea what I wanted to be. I thought vaguely of being an actress. But it seemed automatic that I went on to university, so I studied history; it and English had been my best subject as school.

> At school I was best at languages. I was particularly interested in art, but was advised not to carry on with it because of the lack of career prospects. I had no formal careers guidance, although an assistant headmistress was very influential in helping me to decide to read psychology.

> It was automatic that I should go to university. By far my best subject at school was geography. I remember once seeking out vocational guidance from the careers office and saying that what I wanted to do was write for the *National Geographic* magazine. I was told that such people were employed only on a freelance basis and to go away and think about something else. I thought vaguely about being a vet but was advised against it by my parents, who said I would not be strong enough to deliver cows! I also thought vaguely of being a teacher . . . I saw university as simply another stage in my educational ladder, and studied geography.

Most believed that they made largely unfettered decisions. As may be seen from the present occupations noted after each extract, however, their initial choices were often very different from their career patterns in later life. Chance played a significant role in a number of decisions:

My best subjects at school were English and history. There was minimal
careers guidance, but it seemed automatic that I would go on to university.
My original career thought was to be an archivist, and I applied to Durham
University for a place but was rejected. In the middle of that summer, with
no other applications, under consideration, I was unsure what to do, when a
relative who was a lawyer suggested law. First degrees in law were just
coming in at Scottish universities. I applied for a place and was accepted.
(law)

I was very keen on music, especially the piano. My first choice of career
would have been to go to music college. I applied, but was not offered a
place. As a fallback, I had also applied to university to read German, so I
started a degree in German. (industry)

In a few cases, there was already a clear commitment to a vocation
which the interviewee would follow throughout her professional life:

I grew up in a medical environment and became more and more interested
in, and committed to, medicine as a teenager. So it seemed a natural thing
to go on to study medicine at university. (health)

More characteristically, however, career thoughts were, as one
interviewee phrased it, 'muddy', and many schoolgirls chose simply to
read for general arts degrees:

I hated school. I received very little careers guidance. I left with the idea that
I wanted to work with people. At that point I had no particular ambition. So
I studied for an ordinary arts degree.

I had no career thoughts at school. My father suggested the civil service, so
I went to Oxford to read classics.

In a number of cases, interviewees experienced pressure from parents or
schools to limit their choices to ones thought to be appropriate for
women:

I was all-round at school, doing both arts and science. I was stronger in arts
but enjoyed science. I was very keen to be a doctor, but both my parents
totally disapproved. My father thought it was totally unsuitable for a girl.
My mother felt strongly that I was going to be taking a place away from a
boy, that the government would spent a lot of money training me to be a
doctor and then, of course, I would have to stop once I got married. It was
therefore a total and utter waste of government money and it was slightly
immoral of me even thinking of being a doctor. In my final year at school,
they agreed that I could apply for one place in medicine, with the rest in
arts. I failed to get the place in medicine, so they said, 'That's it — you're
going to do an arts degree.' So I did.

The choices then if you were a girl were nursing or teaching. I wondered about being a dental hygenist, but the local careers guidance officer suggested that teaching would be a better career. When I left school I took a job as a clerical worker, but I still hankered after dental hygiene.

I left school with five highers — English, French, Latin, history and mathematics. I had no careers advice at school, but my mother, a very strong character, advised me to go to [a college which trained teachers of domestic science]. My years were not very enjoyable. I disliked many of the subjects, but I was interested in teaching.

More often, however, interviewees were unaware of gendered presumptions about fields of study, or they actively fought against them:

It simply never occurred to me that being a girl might limit my choice of a career. But I did know for certain that I would never be a teacher — partly because so many people seemed to assume that teaching was something which girls did.

At school it was taken for granted that one would go on to university. But there was no gender bias. Anyone who wanted to do law or medicine was encouraged to do so.

Other types of parental or school pressures were also sometimes actively and successfully countered:

My strongest subjects at school were physics and applied maths. My mother worked as a part-time secretary, and my father was keen that I should train as a bilingual secretary. But I had always wanted to teach, so I went to university with that in mind to do a BSc in physics and statistics.

At school English, history and geography had been my best subjects, but I was interested in a possible career in marine biology. I had been good at science at school, but not at mathematics. My love of the outdoors and my liking for activity made me think of the navy: I was keen to go into Wrens education; their lifestyle appealed to me. But my father was not keen and wanted me to go to university instead. I agreed with him that I would go to university for one year and that, if I passed, I would leave and join the Wrens. So I did.

The subjects which our interviewees chose to study in higher education formed a reasonable cross-section of academic interests, although they were clustered predominantly in the arts at both honours and general degree level:

Figure 19

UNDERGRADUATE COURSES

	%
Arts	40
Social Sciences	18
Sciences	18
Law	8
Education	8
Medicine/Nursing	5
Hotel Management	3
Secretarial Studies	3

No. of Interviewees = 40

In the next section of this chapter we shall consider further some of the implications of these choices and their effect on interviewees' years in higher education. Meanwhile, let us look for a little at the greatly contrasting experience of those who left school to enter paid employment.

CHOOSING PAID EMPLOYMENT

A total of nine of our interviewees left school to enter paid employment directly rather than continue with studying. In making this decision, the major pressure which they now recall was economic, and there appears rarely to have been much encouragement from their schools for them to do otherwise:

> I left school at fifteen and went into an office, because I needed to earn money.

> At school I did reasonably well and enjoyed bits of it. My strength lay in working with figures, especially in maths and accountancy. In fourth year, while preparing to sit O grades, I decided to leave. Looking back, I wonder how I came to the decision but at the time it seemed like a good idea. My sister, who was one year older, had left school, had a job and used to come home and tell me about the excitement of working in Glasgow and having some money to spend at the weekends. This gave me the idea of looking about. At that stage jobs were very easy to come by. I talked to my parents about it. My father was quite happy at my leaving school, although my mother would have preferred me to have stayed on. When I mentioned to the school that I was leaving, no encouragement was given to me to change my mind. I applied for various jobs and eventually took one with an accountancy firm as an office junior.

In two cases, interviewees left school qualified to enter higher education. But they chose not to do so, for very different reasons:

I left school with Highers at sixteen. I loved horses: they were my life outside of school. So I trained in horse management, but there were no career prospects. My parents suggested a secretarial course, which also did not appeal. So I worked in a hotel for a year.

I liked school and did well. I wasn't particularly good at maths and sciences, but I loved English and art; one of my English teachers was particularly influential and introduced me to the beauty of literature. I left school with five Highers. My first career choice would have been teaching, but it was financially impossible for my family to send me to university. My second choice was journalism, so I got an apprenticeship with a local newspaper.

Most characteristically, they undertook non-manual routine work:

I did well academically at school and was especially good at languages and maths. I left at fifteen to do a secretarial course, where I won a prize for commercial subjects. My first job was as a book-keeper in a local shop.

I was extremely good at English, not so good at maths. I was put into the secretarial stream. When I was fifteen, my father suggested that I should leave and do office work. My sister had also left early — to join the Wrens. When I left, I got a job as an office junior, and learnt shorthand for three evenings a week.

I left school after sixth year, but my results weren't good enough to go to university. So I spent a year being unemployed and then got a job as a copy typist in an office.

We shall follow the career paths of all of these employed young women in Chapter 3. Meanwhile, it is indicative of the role played by education in the lives of our interviewees that, in all but two cases, this group of school leavers returned later to education as mature students. Most often they entered university, but they sometimes undertook professional training.

The choices of courses as mature students were dramatically different both from those who had proceeded directly to higher education and, interestingly, also from mature female students as a whole in Scotland. As we have seen above, those of our interviewees who went directly on to undergraduate study were concentrated in the arts, sciences and social sciences. Gerver (1990) shows that most female mature students in Scotland tend to enter education, followed by the arts and social sciences. By contrast, none of our interviewees who became mature students studied for an arts, a pure science or social science degree. Rather, they chose law, civil engineering, banking and management and business studies; one chose education but hated it and moved as soon as possible into an accountancy apprenticeship.

The directly vocational and applied nature of these choices is far more typical of male mature students. The motivations mentioned for such choices are also more characteristic of male than female clusters of motivations for learning as adults (Munn and MacDonald, 1988). As we shall see later, our interviewees generally — particularly those who became undergraduate mature students — are far from being masculine in their personal or their professional lives; all but one of those who were undergraduate mature students are or have been married; most have children, and most tend to believe that women have different management styles from men. It is likely that their unusual choices of what to learn as adults reflect both their high levels of vocational commitment as well as the highly pressurised lives which they lead, which leave them unable to spare much time for learning for its own sake.

In Chapter 3 we shall explore further the factors which led them to such decisions. Meanwhile, let us return to the majority of our interviewees, those who, having made more conventional choices, went directly from school to higher education. How far did they grow at university? What new elements entered their lives? And what factors shaped their choice of where they would go after graduation?

Choices at university

Of those of our interviewees who went directly from school into higher education, by far the greatest number (89 per cent) went to university, while the others did professional training. Virtually all of them completed their courses successfully. But the similarity of patterns of experience ends there.

To begin with, our interviewees are divided almost equally between those who studied honours and those who undertook general degrees: sixteen took honours degress, while seventeen did general or ordinary degrees. Both their reasons for this choice and its consequences, particularly in their first destinations after graduation, are worth examining.

A number of women never considered anything other than a general degree:

> I was the only person in my family to go to university. I did an ordinary MA and found it easier than I expected. But I never had any great aspirations for myself; it never occurred to me to do an honours degree.

Others were aware of the possibility of reading for honours, but rejected it, most typically for social reasons:

I went to university with a group of school friends who also all did ordinary degrees. We were all asked to do honours but all refused. I personally made the decision because I didn't feel strongly committed to my two main subjects — history and archaeology. It was the fashion to do an ordinary degree.

I took four years to do an ordinary degree. The reason was partly to do with my active social life and partly because of the work which I did in politics and journalism.

The choice not to read for honours was occasionally linked to a feeling about the sexual undesirability of appearing to be academically successful:

When I was at university I don't remember ever discussing male-female roles. But I was conscious of an assumption that girls became less sexually desirable if they did well academically — you didn't want that stamp on you.

Decisions were also made on other grounds of immediate interest rather than long-term goals:

I was a bit over-awed at university and never made much impact. I worked very hard. I was going to do an honours degree, but I saw a job as the head of the economics department in [an organisation]. I was advised against applying for it by my academic tutors, but I did apply and got the job.

Of those who chose to read for honours, most appeared to be motivated, at least in part, by a high level of personal commitment to their chosen field as well as by the fact that academic success seemed to come easily to them. Only once did an interviewee directly express her academic ambition:

At school academically successful girls — particularly those who had worked hard to succeed — were seen as only compensating for social failure; it was the "boys don't make passes at girls who wear glasses" syndrome. At university I revelled in the sudden freedom to do as well as I could, so I read for an honours degree, partly for the sheer pleasure of academic success!

As we shall see in more detail in Chapter 3, there appears to have been a fairly substantial effect of the kind of degree on interviewees' subsequent professional lives in the short term, and to a lesser extent, in the long term as well. Those with honours degrees seemed to be much more likely than those with ordinary degrees to begin and to continue to work in areas where their academic expertise was directly relevant. In many cases, those with ordinary degrees seemed as uncertain about their intellectual

commitments when they graduated as when they had become under-
graduates, and they typically experimented with a number of possibilities
before beginning to build their professional expertise in one or two main
areas of interest. Even those who had done ordinary degrees in such
directly vocational fields as law often decided not to practice in the subject
of their first degree. But some of the honours graduates also made major
shifts in their intellectual commitment after graduation: a chemist became
an accountant; a psychologist moved into banking; an economist went on
to train as a secretary; and a physicist proceeded to take a second degree in
politics and economics.

GROWING UP AT UNIVERSITY

Regardless of the kind of degree which they finally chose, most of our
interviewees enjoyed their years at university as their intellectual and
social experiences grew:

> It was only during my first year at university that it occurred to me that I
> could study what I really most cared about rather than what other people
> thought would be most socially responsible. So I made a drastic change from
> science to arts, from studying what I thought was my duty to learning about
> what I loved.

> I was one of only three pupils from my year at school to go to university that
> year. My horizons greatly broadened.

> It was automatic that I should go to university. I knew I would have a
> career, but I was not particularly ambitious when I left school. At university
> I became clear that I wanted to become responsible for my own financial
> security. I think this stemmed largely from my father's illness and from a
> long cool look at the benefits of my mother's working. I felt that I wanted to
> do the same — to guarantee my own financial independence. Overall I
> simply saw university as another stage in my educational ladder. I enjoyed
> parts of it, and it gave me new ways of thinking and new experiences.

> At university there were only three girls in physics. I was a quiet, shy
> person and was thrown in at the deep end. But I came out at the end much
> more self confident.

> At university I found a very mixed age group — there were many ex-
> servicemen, and American and African students.

> My degree was four years of growing up — there was a great deal of self-
> development on the course.

Most of our interviewees also took part in a large number of extracurricular activities as undergraduates, continuing the same pattern which they had shown at school:

> I was a joiner of societies — at one point I was a member of eighteen different ones! I was a member of the Oxford Socialist Club, of a pressure group for the entry of women to the Oxford Union, and I was active in the National Union of Students, helping to establish their hardship committee. I was also involved in helping to set up Oxfam. So I look back on my university time as being very full.

> University was my first experience of all kinds of intellectual possibilities, and I was intoxicated by it. I joined all kinds of societies, debated, took part in mock parliaments, directed plays, and stayed up until dawn arguing about philosophical issues.

But, for several interviewees, university offered less than they had expected, usually because, lacking careers guidance at school, they had chosen the wrong subject or because they found the course itself educationally suspect:

> University was a big disappointment. I had chosen the wrong course, which I did not find challenging academically, although I enjoyed the social side of university life.

> I enjoyed university but feel that in some ways I squandered the time academically.

> In some ways I enjoyed my course at university, but I felt that the criteria used to assess students were not always educational, and the course itself was not always aimed at drawing people out educationally. We were only regurgitating, rather than using our initiative in thinking.

Most of our interviewees attended British universities at a time when women were noticeably in the minority; only a handful studied at women's colleges. Several spoke about their awareness of a male chauvinist culture amongst the predominantly male academic staff and their feelings of being excluded from part of the life of the university simply because they were female:

> I quite enjoyed life at university but felt discriminated against in some ways by some lecturers, who were clearly more interested in the male students.

> I found university very disappointing. Most of the lecturers were either drunk, lecherous or misogynists.

> Seventy students a year read physics, of whom ten each year were women. The professor interviewed every female applicant!

While a number reported that they found few problems in being a woman at university, for at least one interviewee there were obvious conflicts between her expectations for herself as a woman and as an aspiring professional:

> I can remember the odd late night discussion at university, when I used to argue heatedly (I was engaged at the time) in favour of biologically pre-determined roles. I also believed that I would always both work and raise a family, and that my being female would have no effect on my professional life. Consistency and awareness of the real world played little part in my thinking!

LEAVING UNIVERSITY

The initial patterns of all our interviewees' choice of first employment will be considered in depth in Chapter 3. Before returning to the whole group of fifty women, however, it is worth noting briefly the characteristic trends amongst the largest group — those who graduated from university.

As they prepared to leave university, most of our interviewees lacked any specific strategy. Although their vocational decision-making became much more structured as they grew older, most seemed to be drifting at the stage when they finished university. The 'milk round' was a typical way of finding a first employer, who almost invariably was quickly replaced by another:

> In my final year at university I accepted a post with Proctor and Gamble through the milk round.

> My first job was via the milk round, for Plessey.

> I went to the university careers advisory service, who were moderately helpful. I then applied for numerous banking jobs through the milk round, and joined the Royal Bank in their graduate training scheme.

For one undergraduate, the very source of advice proved so attractive that she opted for it:

> I enjoyed university both academically and socially. I had no long-term career plans, so I went to the university careers service for advice. I had been thinking vaguely of social work but I then decided that careers guidance was a useful job in itself, so I went to train as a careers guidance officer!

The general trend amongst our interviewees as they applied for their first jobs is summed up in an extract from one of them:

When I left university I had no ambitions and I was not competitive. But I had always assumed that I would work for the rest of my life.

Occasionally gendered expectations played an important part in making the choice (seen later as highly flawed) of a first destination:

> I didn't know what I wanted to do after university. My father said that I ought to go into management, but at that point management was only a word to me; I had only a very brief knowledge and understanding of what was meant by the term. Most people got jobs easily at the end of the course. Especially the boys seemed to have their lives mapped out for them. I went on to take a secretarial course, which I now regard as a major error.

And, in another case, gender restrictions prevented one undergraduate from pursuing a particular interest:

> I wasn't much conscious of gender as an issue in the late sixties at university. One of the jobs that quite interested me was working as inspector of ancient monuments. But I knew that I couldn't apply because they only took males. I remember my tutor saying that is disgraceful, that's awful. You should be up in arms about this. But I wasn't — I just accepted that I couldn't apply for that.

As we have already noted, however, honours graduates tended to be the exception to the general pattern of initial drifting. Their decisions primarily involved not the fields within which they would work but rather only the particular context within which they would pursue their academic interests:

> One of my professors suggested that I should carry on with research, but I preferred the idea of teaching or entering the scientific civil service. I went on to take my first teaching job at an agricultural college, and did a PhD part-time.

> I don't remember ever wondering very much what I would do after my first degree. I assumed that I would go on to post-graduate study. My only decision was where that should be — whether I should go where my fiancé (who was also going on to post-graduate study) wanted to study, or try for a place at one of the two universities where I particularly wanted to go. I decided to become a married post graduate student.

> I wasn't sure what I wanted to do when I left university. Echoing my interest in history and architecture, I was offered a job in a museum in London, and as a management trainee in Cadbury's. But I was also approached about a scholarship in adult education at Ruskin College, including theory and practice in the field. I applied and got it.

Regardless of the paths they chose, however, those of our interviewees who completed higher education were enacting in practice the beliefs which are held by those of their contemporaries who hold, or hope to hold, senior management positions. In a recent study of policies, practices and attitudes about women in management in Scotland, SIACE (1990) has shown that over half of female employees (compared with only 20 per cent of employers, nearly all of whom were male) believe that 'Women require more qualifications than men to reach the same levels in management'; a substantial majority of both employers and employees believe that 'Women require more drive than men to reach the same level of management.' Those of our interviewees who completed their higher education seem to have been preparing for a future in which they would face greater challenges in their career progression than their brothers, boyfriends and male colleagues.

Looking backwards

Analysis of our interviewees' early lives suggests that a substantial majority came from backgrounds where educational achievement was highly valued and where they were encouraged to make their own decisions. Most showed clear early indications of qualities that would be important in their later lives as increasingly powerful women. Many recalled feelings of being different from their friends; they rebelled against conventional norms of behaviour and thinking; and they tended to identify with the parent perceived to be in charge. They also had a pronounced commitment to religious or political causes, and a love of organising people and events.

Initially, the academic choices of those who proceeded directly to university tended to be highly conventional; the wide range of academic options open to pupils at Scottish schools was only occasionally reflected in our interviewees' choice of undergraduate courses. At the point of entry into higher education, three distinct groups appear to emerge: those early entrants who chose general degrees, most typically in the arts and social sciences; those early entrants who chose honours degrees, also primarily in the arts and social sciences; and those mature entrants who, after leaving school less well qualified than the other two groups, later chose highly vocational courses in higher education. Regardless of the way in which they did it, however, 96 per cent of our interviewees gained higher education qualificiations.

These clusters of characteristics — particularly those relating to levels of education — clearly set our interviewees apart from both men and other women in their generations. But how far do the clusters relate primarily to a Scottish context and how far might they also be true of successful women in other environments?

Miles (1985) has argued that 'the correspondence of powerful women either to the men of power or to the rest of the female population is very limited. But top women correlate well with each other.' In particular, the forty women whom she interviewed tended to share the following characteristics as girls:

● They came from an empowering family, where their mother was out of tune with domestic work and conventional images of motherhood, their father was emotionally warm and seriously committed to his daughter's future, and their grandmother was dynamic.
● Their early lives showed a degree of insecurity and distress — of being out of phase.
● They showed a growing sense of their ability to cope with distress, and, in particular, a sense of being stronger than others, especially of being stronger than men.
● They were high academic achievers.
● They experienced concrete, external success as confirmation of their promise and proof of their worth.
● They showed a strong sense of personal autonomy, self reliance and ability to take on responsibility.

Several of these characteristics — the empowering family, academic achievement and ability to take on responsibility — appear also in the lives of our interviewees. Some of the characteristics of their school lives also resemble closely the patterns of experience which Miles found: like hers, our interviewees often excelled as girls in performance-related activities — such as music, drama or competitive sport — and they showed an early and persistent organising streak. However, the proportion of our interviewees exhibiting certain characteristics is even more pronounced than Miles found in her interviewees. For instance, while 75 per cent of her interviewees were graduates, 96 per cent of ours hold higher education qualifications, normally at graduate level.

In other respects, we found a somewhat different picture from that of Miles. The level of distress which she found in the early lives of her interviewees (and which appears also to characterise highly successful American men) appeared to be considerably lower in our interviewees, who most typically reported stable, secure, nurturing childhoods. Only a minority — albeit a substantial one — of our interviewees reported disturbing factors in their childhood, such as the death of a parent, parental disharmony, or relocations. Moreover, as we shall see in greater depth in Chapters 3 and 4, most of our interviewees did not experience success as confirming their worth. They tended, rather, to view their early success as resulting primarily from chance.

Unlike Miles' interviewees, many of ours reported that they had drifted into higher education and subsequently into their first paid employment, typically without any clear goals and often without a strong sense of ambition. Miles' interviewees appear typically to have chosen to read law, business studies and other highly vocational subjects at university. Those of our interviewees who entered higher education as mature students conformed to this pattern. The majority of our interviewees, however, tended conventionally to read the arts and social sciences, despite the fact that girls from single-sex schools — those attended by over one-third of our interviewees — generally tend to make less traditional subject choices than those from mixed schools (Sarah, Scott and Spender, 1980). A much smaller number of our interviewees opted for the pure and applied sciences or for vocational subjects such as law, medicine or business studies.

Overall, however, our interviewee's experiences and attitudes as girls appear to have much in common with those of other women in senior positions. But we were struck by the extent to which our interviewees' advantages — such as coming from stable home backgrounds and being academic high achievers — appear to be even greater than those found elsewhere, and their disadvantages also proportionately less. If powerful women generally correlate well with each other, as Miles argues, it appears that women in senior positions in Scotland resemble one another to an even greater extent — at least as far as their childhood experiences and attitudes are concerned.

Both as girls and young women, then, the majority of our interviewees closely resemble one another. But these similarities by no means ensure, or even encourage one to predict, that the women who exhibit them will become successful. As they leave university — and, for those who did not proceed directly to higher education, school — our interviewees display ambiguous, often conflicting and contradictory patterns in their lives. Their childhoods have been fundamentally stable and secure, but have sometimes been marked, too, by periods of distress and by highly gendered assumptions about what kinds of choices will be available to them as adults. Overall they are much more highly qualified than the majority of their age cohorts, but these qualifications are typically in liberal rather than vocational subjects. They are accustomed to success in performance-related activities, but their career thoughts are 'muddy', and they tend to view their successes so far as largely a matter of luck rather than of ability. A fairly high proportion, often without any deeply felt desire to become teachers, are considering education as a career. Those who left school to enter paid employment, despite their often good academic record, tend to see in front of them only the need to earn money, often in typically female occupations such as clerical work, for which they feel neither aptitude nor inclination.

How do they then become professors, Lord Provosts, sheriffs, directors, principals, consultants, senior managers, chief executives, editors? In particular, how do they so in a country where, as we have seen in Chapter 1, rising to a senior position as a woman tends to mean blazing a new trail, because there are so few women who have been there before? In Chapter 3 we shall outline the stages by which they moved to their present positions and shall try to identify the major factors involved.

Chapter Three

Career Tapestries

Introduction

Until recently most models of career patterns have been built on assumptions of male managers working predominantly within large organisations. Typically, such studies have identified four major career phases (see, for example, Schein, 1976, and Hunt and Collins, 1983). In the first, exploratory stage, after completing initial full-time education, individuals tend to experiment with a variety of occupations and test different options; this stage lasts until roughly the mid-twenties. In the second stage, lasting roughly until the mid-thirties, there is a building phase, and career routes become more firmly established. The third stage, until about the mid-forties, consists of a period of evaluation, reviewing past achievements and assessing future possibilities. Finally, in the late forties and fifties, comes consolidation, when individuals tend to accept their achieved positions and try to increase their experiences of job satisfaction.

Such models of career-building tend to presuppose that individuals possess or acquire career ambitions from a relatively early age, that career progress upwards in relatively stable and predictable steps, and that the most senior positions are accessible to anyone with sufficient motivation and ability. The last of these assumptions has been widely questioned as far as women are concerned (see, for instance, Marshall, 1984 and SIACE, 1990); the term 'glass ceiling' is increasingly used to express the view that many, if not most, senior management posts are usually not available to women.

How far does the four-stage model of career development hold true for our interviewees? The answer is scarcely at all: in most of the facets of their careers, our interviewees appear to have much less in common with their male counterparts than with one another. In particular, they share with one another the patterns of what one interviewee referred to as 'tapestried' careers — a mosaic of employment patterns created from whatever was nearest to hand, often containing many apparently disparate elements carefully stitched together.

Only a minority of our interviewees have spent their working lives primarily with one major employer:

Figure 20

FREQUENCY OF CHANGE OF EMPLOYER

	%
Most of Career with One Employer	28
Moved Every 4 – 7 Years	62
Moved More Frequently	10

No. of Interviewees = 50

As we shall see later in more detail, some of the reasons for such patterns are connected with gender. Career breaks following childbirth interrupt continuous service with any one employer; the frustrations experienced because of sexual discrimination or harassment have caused some women to leave employers with a particularly bad record on such issues; and partners' geographical mobility has often played a crucial role. But several interviewees also mention that they followed a deliberate policy of changing employers every few years:

> I'm looking for challenge . . . and variety . . . In many ways my present post is ideal, but you shouldn't stay too long in any one place, and I never have. (Education)

Moreover, the working lives of those of our interviewees who became mature students often changed drastically following their completion of higher education. This tendency holds true both for those who, as mature students, became graduates for the first time as well as for those returners who chose entirely different fields of study on their second or even third undergraduate careers.

Apparently abrupt changes in their field of work and their employer are characteristic of a number of our other interviewees as well. Experiments with possible fields of work and likely employers seem to have continued in many cases well beyond early womanhood; thus, one interviewee's career includes lengthy periods of working as a researcher, a lecturer, a journalist, a counsellor and a manager, while another's range includes work in the trade unions, politics and journalism.

Not merely the actual employer but also the industrial sector of employment have varied dramatically for a number of our interviewees. A substantial number have moved between public, private and voluntary sector employers. Others have ranged widely in their types of employer within a single major sector — moving, for example, from local government to various kinds of educational institutions or from manufacturing industry to the media.

Our interviewees also differ from the typical patterns of male colleagues in the ages at which they make major career moves. Following the lengthy period of experimentation in their twenties, our interviewees — most notably but not exclusively those with children — tend not to have major moves upwards in their thirties but rather in their forties and fifties. One major factor in this pattern is the birth of children, which caused a major interruption in the careers of most of our interviewees with children:

Figure 21

CAREER IMMEDIATELY FOLLOWING BIRTH OF FIRST CHILD

	%
Career Break	46
Part-Time Professional Work	25
Full-Time Professional Work	25
Part-Time Non-Professional Work	4

No. of Interviewees = 24

Even for childless interviewees, however, major professional success has tended to come in their forties and fifties rather than, as to so many of their male colleagues, during their thirties. Factors apparently implicated appear to include a late developing awareness of ambition or career potential; reluctance to risk relationships with actual or potential partners for career advancement; the operation of an old boys' network in promotion to senior levels; and the belief, widely held by both sexes, that women have to work harder than men to achieve equal seniority.

Here, as well as in the other factors involved in the career development of our interviewees, gender interacts in a complex way with aspiration and achievement. It is this interaction which form the basis for much of the discussion of career patterns which follows. Before examining the more obviously gender-based factors such as attachment to geographically mobile partners or responsibility for children, however, we shall consider more broadly why our interviewees chose particular careers, why and how they have made major vocational moves both in employment and in education and training, their attitudes towards work and the presence or absence of mentors. We shall then examine in greater detail whether and how far they believe that their career paths have been shaped by gender. Finally, we shall assess, through their own words, how far they feel they have achieved a satisfactory balance in their lives and what they perceive as the main factors in their success.

Career choices

Despite the external diversity of the career development of our interviewees, the reasons for their choice of careers and their attitudes towards their work share a few major characteristics. Many of our interviewees told us how much they care about their work — a feeling often expressed as commitment or even as love:

> I will stay in law for the rest of my life. Sometimes I ask, why am I doing all this? Why am I working the hours that I work? But basically I'm doing it because of the satisfaction I get from it. (Law)

> I don't think I could work successfully in a job unless I believed in what I was doing and unless I loved most of it. It was only when I finally began to work in my present field that I found a lot of opportunities opening up, despite the fact that I had little formal training in it; previously, I had felt in dead-end jobs, even though they were in the academic field in which I had qualified. (Voluntary organisation)

Indeed, some of our interviewees were reluctant to consider future changes once they found work that they specially enjoyed:

> I'm not sure what I shall do in the future. I often think that I should be moving on and away from [the company] but I thoroughly enjoy my work, and I'm quite happy with the level I've reached. (Industry)

> I am not sure where I should like to go now. I'm fairly happy to play the Warwick role and be the power behind the throne. I would probably prefer to stay second in a large [organisation] rather than be chief executive in a smaller one. My only ambition is to remain in a position of influence. (Government)

Typically, however, our interviewees revel in change and deliberately seek it out:

> I love my work, and I enjoy it enormously. But I also believe that you

shouldn't stay in any one post more than seven years or so — otherwise, there's a danger that you will become complacent, and that the cutting edge that shapes new ideas will be dulled. (Voluntary organisation)

A tapestried career is a privilege, not a disadvantage. (Government)

But most of our interviewees believe that, however desirable for the sake of change, their major career moves have been made fortuitously rather than in a planned fashion:

Am I ambitious? Yes and no. I've simply been at the right place at the right time. Things have happened to me rather than my going out to improve my career. (Industry)

My career has never really been fully planned — it just happened. Most of my career moves were made because people had approached me to apply for jobs rather than my feeling the need to move. (Health)

I was very lucky to have been appointed. I would never have thought of applying but was encouraged by various colleagues. (Education)

A handful of our interviewees, however, have taken a more systematic approach to their future careers:

Recently I've become much more conscious of career planning. Up to now my career has just happened. (Voluntary organisation)

Regardless of how it is acquired, however, does power remain, as Miles (1985) has suggested, the last taboo? A number of our interviewees speak openly of their ambition:

I am competitive with myself rather than with other people. If I see an opportunity for something I take it. I am a natural leader. Having a career has always been important to me. (Industry)

But most of those who admit to ambition draw careful boundaries around how far they are prepared to satisfy ambition at all costs:

I am ambitious in a way but I don't want to get on at other people's expense. (Finance)

I am ambitious, but not in terms of a high-paid job with a car. I want to continue working in jobs which I feel are important and in work I can do well. It must also be a worthwhile job. (Voluntary organisation)

Nearly all of those who speak openly of their liking for power emphasise the extent to which they want to use it to initiate change and to improve quality:

> I want to change things . . . I'm very much in favour of empowering the individual. I want to change the way we all are in Scotland. (Industry)

> I like being in charge and I enjoy knowing when things are properly done. (Government)

> I've always had plenty of ideas and like to seem them coming to fruition. I was extremely ambitious for [my organisation] and did a great deal in developing work there and in publicising it. (Education)

> I am ambitious, and (although I know one doesn't usually talk about such things) I both like having power and being seen to have power. But what I like most about my job is that it lets me try all kinds of new ideas, some of which I can see actually have an effect in other people's lives. (Voluntary organisation)

In two cases, interviewees admit a straightforward delight in power for its own sake:

> Yes, I am ambitious. I am a driver. I have been called an autocrat. (Government)

> I love my job, and I am ambitious. I expect a lot from other people — perhaps I should be more tolerant. I'm always under pressure and can't understand why other people aren't like me. (Finance)

One interviewee insists however, that she is neither ambitious nor competitive:

> I've always wanted to work rather than to have a career. I have no ambitions and I'm not competitive, but I always assumed that I would work for the rest of my life. My main motivations for choice have been the attractions of specific jobs rather than considerations of my cv. (Voluntary organisation)

Major career moves

Because of our commitment to our interviewees that interview material would remain anonymous, we are unable to quote many examples of the motivations and circumstances of interviewees' major career moves; such details are so bound up with specific professions and organisations that individuals could too easily be identified. In the discussion which follows, we have therefore drawn on patterns that emerge from analysis of interviewees' career moves, although the direct evidence which we have cited is sometimes thin.

All of the major factors which appear to have shaped interviewees' major career moves appear to be contingent on personal circumstances rather than resulting from systematic planning. One major factor appears to be selection to take part in a project of some kind, which often brought interviewees into contact with more senior staff and which expanded their range of experience. All of those to whom such opportunities occurred subsequently took advantage of them:

> My first junior management appointment was a very crucial one. It was at this stage that I was approached by head office to help undertake a work study of [the organisation] — a very controversial study. There were four of us in the whole team; I was the only woman. It helped me first of all to see the variety of management techniques used in [the organisation] and, perhaps more importantly, get my name known. (Finance)

> Once, to my surprise, I was suddenly asked by [a member of senior management] if I were willing to be seconded to [another organisation] to take on an experimental project designed to bridge two parts of the education world. As it happened, I knew a reasonable amount about one of the sectors, but was entirely ignorant of the second, and said so. I was then told that one of the reasons for my selection was that very ignorance! I accepted the post and had a fascinating year coming into contact with all kinds of people whom I wouldn't normally meet. Shortly after the secondment ended, I applied for, and was appointed to, a post in which my year's experience was invaluable. (Education)

> An amazing number of coincidences and good luck have brought me where I am today. I'm not that brilliant. But I got the chance to work on a variety of new projects which have been influential in my career development . . . One of them brought me into contact with a number of people in senior positions; I was often invited to lunch with various heads of departments. This was crucial in getting into the formal netwok that is so important. (Government)

A second major factor appears to be personal involvement in a specific milieu when such experience was seen as essential for a particular post:

> Part of the reason [for applying] was my involvement in the union when I worked in [an educational institution]. This gave me a lot of links, a lot of contacts with [government]. And I've never been afraid to speak my mind and to challenge things I didn't like. My application was in the form of a

statement of interest which I hadn't expected to be taken seriously. I was absolutely amazed when I was offered the post. (Government)

My interest in politics began because of my involvement in the local community. I would always speak my mind at local meetings. Eventually, someone said, 'If you're so good at getting things done, why don't you go into politics?' (Government)

A third major factor in many interviewees' major career moves is a domestic crisis:

At this stage my marriage was going through a crisis and I thought of leaving my husband — for which I would need financial independence. But at the beginning I had no intentions of having a career.

The most important years in my life were when my marriage broke up. This gave me the opportunity — indeed the necessity — to rethink my life. At this stage I decided to [undertake higher education], partly with the long-term view that it would help my career, partly in the short term to give me something to do with my time.

A fourth major factor in the career moves of some of our interviewees is the decision to continue their education. Motivations to become mature students included a mixture of vocational aspirations with a desire for self-development, although typically both were shaped by family considerations:

I went back to college because I knew I was clever and had missed out. It was for personal development rather than for career development. My first idea was to study home economics because it could lead to a job that would fit in with school holidays. But I would have had to leave [where I lived] to do it, so I started instead to look at what was available where I lived. Law was available, and it was vocational. I didn't want to do a lengthy arts degree followed by further training. (Government)

After staying at home for three years with my children, I started studying for O grades through correspondence courses and then got a job as secretary in [a company], where I was keen to get on. I also did an HNC in secretarial and business studies at evening classes over three years. I was seen as being an extremely good executive secretary, and that infuriated me. So I looked around at what else I might do and thought of studying for an MBA. I was eventually accepted, despite not having a degree. (Industry)

A fifth factor in the career development of a substantial number of our interviewees is their attachment to mentors, whom they believe have both directly and indirectly helped their careers by coaching them informally in significant features of their job, organisational life and career strategies. Before discussing our interviewees' responses to mentoring, however, it is important to note that the majority of our interviewees (56 per cent) do not believe that they have had mentors. This finding is at first somewhat unexpected in the light of the many studies which consistently find that a high proportion of successful women have received help from mentors (see, for example, Hennig and Jardim, 1979; Marshall, 1984; Clutterbuck and Devine, 1987). But it is consistent with other suggestions (Miles, 1985) that traditional systems of mentoring have tended to pass women by and, indeed, may create difficulties for both men and women.

Since our interviewees had to cover so much territory in a relatively short space of time, we did not pursue further the question of why those who had not had mentors had not done so. Possible reasons for not having mentors might have included the relative scarcity of senior women, the apparent reluctance of men to groom women to be their successors and the difficulty of finding a senior man who would accept a woman as his potential professional equal rather than as a sexual partner.

The 44 per cent of interviewees who have had mentors tend to have had more than one senior colleague who fulfilled such a role. The numbers reported typically ranged from two to four, and occasionally even more. To a significant extent, the contact with multiple mentors appears to be a function of the multiple careers with our interviewees report. Scotland being the small world that it is, we also found that a number of interviewees view other interviewees as mentors!

But mentors are not always senior professional colleagues. In a number of cases, interviewees report that one or both of their parents, their husbands or their partners have acted as mentors. As we shall see later in more detail in Chapter 4, the personal lives of a number of our interviewees are closely interwoven with their professional careers. Husbands and parents — particularly fathers — are sometimes in the same or a similar profession as their wives or daughters and are recognised as offering the kind of support traditionally available through professional colleagues.

The use of the term mentor may erroneously imply a deliberate strategic choice. In fact, our interviewees tended to see the effect of other individuals in their careers as important only after their choice of them as men and women with whom they shared common interests, enthusiasms, and, characteristically, commitment to causes or ideas.

There are striking differences in the numbrs of men and women chosen as mentors by our interviewees:

Figure 22

GENDER OF MENTORS

	%
Male and Female	45
Male Only	32
Female Only	9
Sex Unspecified	14

No. of Interviewees = 22

Given the relative paucity of women in senior positions in Scotland, it is perhaps not surprising that the mentors of seven of the interviewees are exclusively male and that only two interviewees report that they have had only female mentors. The most prevalent pattern is for mentors to include both men and women. As we shall see later in Chapter 4, the preferred management styles of our interviewees tend to be inclusive of working with both sexes — a preference also reflected strongly in the choice of mentors.

What role do mentors play? Let our interviewees speak directly:

> One of my early bosses was crucial in my career. He was a typical gardener boss who wanted all his staff to do something. At first when I moved into my present job I couldn't find anyone to give me guidance. More recently I've found two individuals who issue challenges in a way that I like, although the views of each diverge. One of them knows the labyrinths of [the organisation] very well and the other listens supportively. (Education)

> Two male managers for whom I worked at different times in my career were influential. One encouraged me to stand up for myself and the other showed me the importance of organising and motivating people. (Finance)

> There are two people whom I see as my mentors — though I'm not sure that they would agree with that perception of their role! One taught me how to prepare the ground for decision makers before putting proposals forward formally; the other taught me how to achieve consensus for strategic and detailed planning. It's not sheer chance, I think, that both of them believed in what they were doing; that's always been important for me. (Voluntary organisation)

In shaping career patterns, all five of these factors interact, of course, both with levels of education and training qualifications (as we noted in Chapter 2) as well as with more explicitly gender related circumstances such as geographical mobility, the presence of children and sexual discrimination. We shall postpone a detailed analysis of the gender-related management styles of our interviewees until Chapter 4 and the discussion of the interaction of their domestic lives with their career patterns until chapter 5. For now we shall consider how far the gender of our interviewees appears to have shaped — and how far they believe that it has shaped — their career development.

Gender and careers

The interaction of career development with gender takes many complex forms, which flow into nearly all of the issues discussed throughout this book. At the risk of over simplification, we propose to consider now only those gender factors which relate specifically to appointment to new posts. In our discussion below, therefore, we shall report and discuss what our interviewees told us about gender and career paths and the perceived effects of child rearing, partners' geographical mobility and sex discrimination on their careers.

GENDER AND CAREER PATHS

There is widespread agreement amongst both sexes that women generally have to be more able and to work harder than men to reach the same level of career development (see, for instance, SIACE, 1990). This perception is also expressed by many of our interviewees across nearly the full range of professions and areas of work which they represent. In the first place, there are many more stories than we have room to report about straight forward sex discrimination:

> Barriers do exist. I was recently on an interviewing panel for a position on a public body. Eventually a woman clearly came out as the best candidate. It was decided by the interviewing panel — which was exclusively male apart from me — that they would appoint the woman but offer her £4,000 less than they had intended. It was, they said, a good enough salary for a woman to get. I didn't quite know how to respond to that. But as I was new in the job I kept quiet. A year later the woman's salary was reviewed and she was upgraded. (Voluntary organisation)

> I stayed in my first job for three years. The career prospects in the company were not nearly as good as I had hoped, largely because I was a woman. It was a very chauvinistic company. There was only one other female . . . and it was clear from the outset that neither of us were going to be promoted to any high level of responsibility. The manager for whom I worked didn't hide his chauvinism. He, for example, sent his daughter to a state school while sending his son to a fee-paying school. It wasn't, so he kept telling me, worth paying out money just to educate a girl. (Industry)

There are still barriers in society — they're called men. More and more women are becoming attracted to self-employment and, indeed, are being successful at setting up their own business. But there are major difficulties especially at the beginning of such an enterprise. Very often bank managers are still prejudiced against women. It's a great problem for many women to get financial backing for their business. (Education)

Yes, I've been discriminated against, and I've seen many men get to the same level sooner. (Finance)

I wasn't going to apply for the post until I heard that the director had said that 'a woman would not have the resilience needed for the job and even if she did she would probably just get married and leave.' It was like a red rag to a bull. (Government)

I've experienced sex discrimination at two job interviewees. At one of them the principal officer concerned said that there was no point in appointing me because I would be pregnant within a year. I said I certainly would not. He said, if not, he would be up to see my husband. At another time I was asked if I realised that I wouldn't be home at five o'clock to make my husband's tea every night and what would my husband's attitude be to that? The same interviewer asked the male candidate whether he took a drink. When he said yes, he did, he was told that was great, you'll fit in well here. And he got the post. (Government)

Many barriers do still exist for women. Although a number [of women] are to be found in the media, they are corralled into particular areas. For example, I once wanted to move into directing but found that as a female it was very difficult to be accepted. Men have a natural and systematic advantage in their careers. (Media)

There are still many barriers for women. It's very hard for career-orientated women who wish to make a good career for themselves in medicine. (Health)

So how have our interviewees dealt with sex discrimination? Overwhelmingly, they have deliberately not sought the legal redress available:

I've heard through feedback from interviews in two different institutions that there was sex discrimination against me on the part of the largely or entirely male appointments committees. On another occasion, I strongly suspected that my male head of department ensured that I would not be promoted within his department. But in none of these cases did I ever seriously consider going to a tribunal. Any case would be very difficult, consisting largely of hearsay. More importantly for me, it would have been professional suicide to take such institutions to a tribunal. But I've always felt guilty that, by not taking the cases to a tribunal, I have not helped other women as much as I should. (Voluntary organisation)

Another reason for not pursuing employers through the courts may well be the belief, held by many of our interviewees, that such discrimination is endemic and systemic, often bound up with an old boys' network:

It's very significant that there are so few women at senior level in education in Scotland. Like goes for like. Job descriptions are very often drawn up with a particular person — who just happens to be male — in mind . . . Intervening at the interview stage is too late. More has to be done at the job description stage to make sure that more women are eligible to join short leets for jobs. (Education)

Many women get stuck at middle management posts because there is a myth — kept going by men — that the top job is always harder. (Education)

While acknowledging that it is typically more difficult for women to reach senior positions, most of our interviewees tend to believe that both men and women are implicated in the fact that there are relatively small numbers of women in senior positions:

I still think that for a woman to have a good career path and be promoted she has to be better than a man. Women have to be much more determined and need the extra dimension which, I regret to say, is not always there with women. I admire women who get up and go. (Education)

Women see things too subjectively and take criticisms of their work to be criticisms of themselves. Women have to start to differentiate between their work and themselves. (Government)

There are still barriers — there are natural male networks and also women's own social attitudes. Women do have a more difficult and tortuous path to the top than men and women have to strive for every job that they get. (Finance)

A major cause of there being so few women in senior positions is women's cultural background, which leads them to very low career aspirations . . . It is an uphill struggle for a woman. I have to prove myself and much more is expected of me than a male in a similar position. (Industry)

In particular, our interviewees identify a number of what they see as characteristically female qualities which militate against promotion to senior positions:

Women tend to understate their abilities. (Media)

Being a woman hasn't ever held me back. If women beaver away, they will get there — the same as men. But it's easy for women to get side-tracked. I'm disappointed at what appears to be the lack of ambition amongst some of the women I deal with. (Finance)

I don't think I've been hindered by being female — in some ways it's helped me . . . To a certain extent women are their own worst enemies. They're often too hesitant. (Education)

I am very much of the opinion that if you have a well-organised and a well-balanced argument, you will win it. Women often do not do their homework. It's very much an all or nothing thing with a woman — they're not prepared to compromise. (Health)

Lots of women use their sex as an excuse for failure. I've never suffered from any form of sexual discrimination . . . Lots of women seem to change their minds — one minute wanting a career and one minute not. Men tend to be more patient as far as their careers are concerned, whereas women want things to happen now and, if they don't, blame their sex for their failure. (Finance)

If they are ambitious, women can get on. But a job is of secondary importance to many women. (Media)

Institutional barriers no longer exist for women. But social attitudes are internalised by women, and women often blame gender for their failure. Being a woman can possibly help — men tend to be more chivalrous and often unduly impressed. Women are often too honest and open, too willing to admit their weaknesses, lacking in self-confidence and not political enough. (Self employed)

There is here a striking difference between the group of interviewees who tend to blame their own sex for its difficulties and the rather larger group who see social expectations and male domination as contributory factors. Analysis of the career patterns and the professions of our interviewees, however, shows no correlation between their views about the reasons for the relative lack of women in senior positions and the characteristics of their own career development.

The only connections which we have established lie, not surprisingly, in political allegiances. Those women who have been brought up in predominantly conservative households are significantly more likely to blame women as individuals for their failure to reach senior positions, while those who grew up in socialist homes tend to see systematic male domination at the root of the problem. As we shall explore further in Chapter 6, there also appears to be a close connection between those women who blame other women for lack of progress and those who express a lack of interest in fostering the careers of other women.

Despite the different clusters of attitudes, however, there are shrewd assessments of the career advantages of being a woman in the male-dominated levels of senior positions:

> Being a woman has sometimes helped. People start with low expectations of me and therefore it is easier to impress. (Government)

> If you are a woman and if you are in a minority, you don't stand out. And therefore being a woman in a man's world does sometimes help. (Media)

In a few cases, interviewees cite examples of positive discrimination in promotion:

> Being a woman has helped at certain stages of my career. There *was* positive discrimination when I was appointed to [one post]. (Education)

> Of course I can't prove it, but it looks to me as if being a woman has increased the likelihood of my being appointed to various public bodies — there simply aren't many other senior women in my field from which to choose! (Voluntary organisation)

A very few of our interviewees (all in government) also believe that their being married women increased rather than decreased the range of choices available to them:

> I don't think it's made much difference to me, being a woman. In fact the big advantage that I've had is that my husband has always earned a good wage, . . . which has give my choice as to whether I needed or wanted to work. (Government)

> As a woman I've had choice — whether to work or not to work and, secondly, whether to keep working. (Government)

A number of our interviewees also recognise that their chances for career development were strongly enhanced by their entering their respective fields at a professional level rather than at lower levels. Their perceptions of such advantages are confirmed by other recent research which suggests that women employees in Scotland tend to receive much less training than their male counterparts (Nelson, 1989) and that employers in Scotland tend not to conduct staff appraisals of their non-managerial staff — the grades in which most women work (SIACE, 1990).

A lot of men don't like to think of women in senior positions. But it's easier for professional women to move up the ladder than for women at, say, supervisory level. But women very often are not prepared to go out and sell themselves. (government)

There also appears to be broad agreement that particular professional fields — notably law and computing — may now offer genuinely equal opportunities to women, despite past discrimination:

More women should come into computing — it's an extremely good career for women. (Industry)

There is no real discrimination in my profession. At the end of the day it comes down to ability, especially as an advocate. You are only as good as your last case. Whether you are male or female is irrelevant. (Law)

I saw major strides being made by women during my years in . . . law . . . They are now reaching the dizzy heights of partnership. But being a partner in a legal firm is a bit like a marriage — it's difficult to get into and difficult to get out of. This causes problems for women who wish to take a career break. (Law)

As the last comment suggests, however, the effect of gender on career development extends much more widely than sex discrimination in its many and richly varied forms. For the twenty-four of our interviewees who have children, there have been major effects on their career development.

CAREER PATTERNS AND CHILDREN

As we have noted earlier in this chapter, the career paths of those of our interviewees with children have tended to follow any one of three main patterns: 46 per cent took a career break, while all but one of the others worked professionally either full-time (25 per cent) or part-time (25 per cent) following the birth of their children. On the whole, those who already held higher education qualifications before having their first child were significantly more likely to work immediately afterwards, while those who were not so qualified tended to take a full career break. Factors in deciding which of the three options to choose included observation of the lives of women at home with children, a sense of moral obligation to give full-time attention to their children, and a delight in young children. But for some there was no perceived choice at all. One interviewee was indignant event at the question of whether she had worked after her children were born. 'No, no,' she insisted.

On the whole, those who took career breaks were happy that they had done so:

> I'm glad that I managed to be at home with my children when they were young. I would recommend to all women to stay at home until their children are at least five.

> I would recommend women to have the confidence to take breaks and to believe that things will work out for you.

In several instances, however, the reality of being at home full-time with young children sent mothers out to look, not so much for careers, as for almost anything to take them away from home and to earn money:

> When my son was six months, I went back to work, partly for financial reasons, partly because I was bored in the house.

> I soon found myself extremely bored and worked on a freelance basis typing and editing documents. My husband and I then decided to set up a small printing business.

Even amongst those who would now recommend career breaks for other women, a substantial number undertook further study during an early stage in their children's development:

> When we moved to [England] I decided to return to study to expand my mind. So I enrolled in an external degree with the University of London.

> When we moved to Edinburgh after the birth of our second child, I enrolled in Telford College because I still hankered after my missed education.

At the opposite end of the spectrum, for those who undertook full time work following the birth of their children, the decision to continue working often evolved over a period of time:

> The idea of my having an on-going career gradually evolved. I was part of a group of women who had all been working for so many years and then would all have families. Then I looked at them and thought, 'Gosh, do I really want to do this?' when I saw the nappies and the bottles and the haggard look in their faces. And I thought, maybe this isn't such a good idea. So I think my friends who were having children at that stage actually acted as a means of influencing me in a negative rather than a positive way.

> When I was pregnant with my first child, I took maternity leave and swithered about whether to return. My job with its restrictions and lack of flexibility offered problems, as did the need for evening work, so there were practical considerations against. No part-time posts were available. But in favour was the fact that I couldn't get back to the same level of post again directly if I left, so I thought, 'It's a lot to give up.' It was really [my

husband] who persuaded me to give it a go. He was the one who said, 'Try it and if it doesn't work, you'll know it hasn't worked.' So I advertised for a nanny and started back.

But what of the experience of the 52 per cent of our interviewees without children? 35 per cent of those without children are single. As we shall see in more detail in Chapter 5, both they and most of their married childless counterparts perceive formidable obstacles in the way of mothers continuing to work at a professional level:

I admire women who can have successful careers and raise well balanced children. I know very few women who have managed to do this.

I'm not sure whether women can have marriage and a family and a career. My friends who are trying to do so can feel very tired and very ragged.

Despite the fact that choices about children have had profound effects on their lives, the career development of those of our interviewees with and without children does not appear to differ significantly, with the minor exception that those who took career breaks and those who worked part-time have postponed their professional advancement until slightly later than their childless or full-time working counterparts. The only significant pattern to emerge is the often regretted choice of part-time work:

When I knew I was pregnant with my first child, I daydreamed about combining being at home with the baby and continuing my academic work. So I resigned from my full-time lectureship and took two part-time jobs instead. On one wonderful day, shortly after my son was born, I sat down to finish writing a research paper while he was sleeping. For a short while I believed that I had the best of both worlds. But soon the realities of badly paid and isolated part-time academic work, together with my intense dislike of housework, sent me out in search of a full-time post and a nanny.

Brook, Jowell, and Witherspoon (1989) have suggested that 'women who have part-time paid jobs may have the worst of both worlds, extra responsibilities outside the home and only limited sharing of activities within it . . . Households in which the woman has a part-time job are more or less indistinguishable from those in which the woman is not in paid work at all.' We shall consider the question of household division of labour in greater detail in Chapter 5. Meanwhile, it is indicative of the unsatisfactory nature of the often advocated solution of part-time work that almost none of our interviewees continued part-time employment for more than a few years.

Cartoon by Viv Quinlan

GEOGRAPHICAL MOBILITY

The importance of decisions about geographical mobility cannot be over-estimated in its effect on the career patterns of both men and women. Irvine and Martin (1986), for instance, suggest that the divergence in career paths between female astronomers and their male counterparts 'occurred fairly rapidly after the first job, as the demands of their husband's career severely restricted the employment choices available to the women.' Striking differences in enforced and chosen mobility as between male and female appear consistently in studies. Kashket et al (1974) found that '93 per cent of the women doctorates answered that they would move only if their husbands obtained a satisfactory position first. In contrast, 83 per cent of men doctorates indicated that they would move whether or not their professional wives had satisfactory prospects for employment.' Sutherland (1985) also notes that, amongst academic

Cartoon by Viv Quinlan

staff, 'one of the major problems for both husband and wife . . . is that of finding posts for them both in the same place . . . The fashion has been for the wife to move when the husband found a new appointment.' Analogously, Scase and Goffee (1989) found that only 10 per cent of married male managers but 50 per cent of married female managers consider that their partners' jobs are very important in deciding whether to move to further their career prospects.

To a large extent, such findings reflect the fact that senior women, if they are married, tend to be married to partners of roughly equal professional standing (Rapoport and Sierakowski, 1982), whereas the same is not true of senior men. The impact of this gender-related factor in the lives of the women whom we interviewed is usually substantial — and devastating.

By far the largest proportion of those of our interviewees who were or are married report leaving their initial or an early job to follow their husband's career moves. The pattern is especially characteristic of those women who took career breaks or worked part time after the birth of their children:

> I always thought I would get married, and I did so when I was twenty-five, by which time I had already worked for five years after graduation. My husband was [a university lecturer] and we went straight to the United States after we were married. I worked professionally there. When we returned I worked part-time professionally until the birth of our first child. Then we moved to [England], and I returned to study part-time, doing an external degree. When we returned to Scotland I worked part-time professionally.

> My first job was chosen solely on a geographical basis, to enable me to live with my husband, to whom I was newly married. I had been offered a post at [a university] but turned it down and instead applied for jobs within easy reach of where my husband was lecturing. Shortly afterwards we moved [abroad], where my husband had been offered a visiting professorship. I then worked at the university to which he had been appointed for two years, after which we moved to Scotland, where he had been offered another university post. Once again, I looked for jobs that were within geographical reach.

There are candid acknowledgements of the mobility problems created by marriage:

> By and large my marriages have helped my career. But if I were single I would be much more mobile. This could be a problem in the future if I want promotion.

> I was working for a job I loved in London when I got married. My husband didn't want to move to London, so we agreed that I would apply for jobs in Glasgow. But if I had been free my preference would have been to move to another job in London.

The pattern of both partners moving to accommodate male jobs, however, appears to be changing. A number of our interviewees comment on ways in which families have taken account of the career needs of both partners. In a very few instances, neither husband nor wife wanted to move from the part of Scotland where they now lived, so mobility was not in itself a problem. More often, however, professional couples have agreed to part-time dual site marriages as the only solution to the geographically conflicting demands of their careers:

> When my husband moved to [England], his firm said that they could find work for me and asked what I did and how much I earned. When he told

them, they quickly changed their mind. Now he works in [England] and I work in Scotland; we meet at weekends.

When a new job at [my present institution] became available, I was invited to apply. At first I said it was impossible: my husband was based in England, and I had an elderly, very demanding mother whom I felt I could not leave. But I was finally persuaded to apply. When I was offered the job, after much soul searching I accepted it. My husband was and always has been very supportive. I moved to [Scotland], renting a flat temporarily and for a few weeks I didn't tell my mother that I had moved! I now feel much more settled. My husband may move up to be with me in the near future. We see each other once every few weeks — it works reasonably well.

Nevertheless, as far as we could tell, in only one instance did a male partner make a career decision partly on the grounds of our interviewee's own career development.

Our decisions about whether and where to move were not always based only on his career. At one point he turned down a fellowship at Oxford partly because we both judged that it would have been much more difficult for me to move at that stage of my career.

As we shall see further below, the presence of partners and children has interacted very significantly with the careers of our interviewees. For many women, decisions about geographical mobility have focused most clearly — and often most cruelly — the conflicts which characterise their lives. Nevertheless, the characteristic of their lives which emerges most compellingly from our interviews is not conflict, but rather balance.

Balance in life

The question of balance in one's life is an issue for virtually all of our interviewees. They are highly conscious of the extent to which the various demands on their energy, time, thought and emotional resources can, and at times do, conflict with one another. Nevertheless, most of our interviewees believe that they should, and do, cope creatively and successfully with the various inter-related facets of their lives:

Several years ago [medical] problems meant that I was off work for several months. It made me rethink my life to a large extent. I know that the problem could return. I'm therefore very keen to have a good balance in my life and not be totally committed to my work.

I don't think I'm highly ambitious. I wouldn't describe myself as having to get to the top of any particular tree. And I think as I get older I'm also more aware of the importance of having a balance in my life. The kids have still got a lot of growing up to do.

Overall I'm happy with the balance in my life — I go to aerobics classes; I travel throughout Europe. But I know that I don't always cope very well. Sometimes I shout and am bad tempered with the children.

One major strategy for creating balance consists of intertwining work with home commitments:

It's difficult to separate work from home. I've lots of extra-work commitments, really because they interest me. I have a social life — when I fit it in.

I find it difficult to separate work from my personal life: the two are very closely intertwined and both are very influenced by religion. I feel that both my life and my career are in God's hands; I have to wait to see what God wants me to do.

I find it difficult to say where the separation lies between my life at work and at home: much of what I read for pleasure is directly relevant to my job; many of my friends share my interests at work, and so on. I like the sense of one part of my life nourishing the other.

For a few women, the exceptionally large demands made on their professional time create problems which, however, they remain determined to solve:

I work too hard, and it takes up too much of my time. The balance isn't right in my life, but I do try and work on it . . . And I do hope it will change in the future.

Perhaps surprisingly, these patterns appear to be as true of those who were married as one of those who were not, and to apply equally to those who had children as to those who did not. In only one case does an interviewee use the word 'guilt' in referring to the balance between her life at work and at home:

I wonder whether my problems [at home] are due to my working. I am concerned about the fact that my mother wants me to stop working and, indeed, expects it of me. I would very much welcome a counselling service for women who are in senior positions and who are often faced with double dilemmas and problems concerning balancing and combining their work and personal life.

But, for those interviewees who are single parents, no strategy can overcome the fact that demands invariably exceed the time available. Only once their children are grown up does this group see the possibility of creating a balance in their lives which allows for more than domestic responsibilities, work commitments and exhaustion.

> It has not been easy being a single parent . . . I'm struggling to create a balance in my life. I hope that in the future I can get a balance that allows me to spend more time with my daughter.

> I've found bringing up two children alone and working full-time extremely difficult. For many years I was drained of energy.

It is perhaps worth noting that our interviewees who are single parents have not chosen deliberately to become so; the circumstances arose through separation, divorce or death. We have alreay seen that other factors have also often limited the choices of our interviewees, such as enforced or unavailable geographical mobility and sex discrimination in promotion. Running through the interviewees, however, is a strong sense of women who feel in charge of their own lives, who feel able to decide whether and how to create a better balance, and whether and how to continue their career development. The exceptions to this powerful sense of self determination are the accounts given to us of why interviewees felt that they had succeeded. It is to this apparent anomaly that we now turn.

Perceived reasons for success

There appear to be three different orders of reasons for their success as our interviewees perceive them. The reasons cited most frequently are (multiple answers were recorded):

Figure 23

MAIN REASONS CITED FOR SUCCESS

	%
Luck or Opportunity	53
Hard Work	22
Qualifications	20

No. of Interviewees = 36

Figure 24

SUBSIDIARY REASONS CITED FOR SUCCESS

	%
Visibility	8
Determination	8
Wide Experience	8
Ambition	8
Competitiveness	6
Help from Family	6
Help from Mentor	6

Figure 25

ADDITIONAL REASONS CITED FOR SUCCESS

Courage to become Self-Employed
It's in God's Hands
Professional Pride
Making the System Work for me
Grit
Having Innovative Ideas
Break-Up of Marriage
Ability
Women's Previous Experience of Working
Performance
Image

Amongst the many different reasons cited by our interviewees for their success so far, only one is mentioned by over 50 per cent of the thirty-six women who replied directly to the question — luck, favourable circumstances or a fortuitous opportunity which was immediately seized upon:

> I've been very lucky in my career. To a certain extent my success can be attributed to being in the right place at the right time. (Education)

> I was really very lucky. There were lots of jobs when I graduated and also lots of child care available. (Voluntary organisation)

Perceptions of luck or chance as the major factor appear to be consistent across a wide range of backgrounds: women working in industry are as likely to cite luck as women in the public or voluntary sectors. Only women in the media (who rarely cite any reason for their success in the first place) do not mention it as a significant factor.

In modestly citing luck or chance, our interviewees share a common perception with nearly all other senior women (see, for instance, Marshall, 1984; Miles, 1985), as well as with women in general, in accounting for success. Given strong social sanctions against immodest women, it is probably impossible to disentangle how far such expressed reasons reflect inner feeling and how far they merely represent prescribed social behaviour. Strikingly, however, our interviewees do not mention the factor in success most often cited by female managers in Scase and Goffee (1989) — performance and results. It appears that modesty may again have been at work or merely that our interviewees simply assume effectiveness to be a sine qua non.

The fact that only 22 per cent of interviewees cite hard work as a reason for success needs to be set beside the fact that nearly all of our interviewees acknowledge at various moments that they work very hard. A characteristic, and much heard comment is:

> I've always been a hard worker — I'm probably a workaholic now. (Industry)

To some extent, it appears as if our interviewees may view such hard work merely as a prerequisite for success rather than any kind of explanation in its own right. Their commitment to long hours of work also has significant implications for their private lives, as we shall consider later in Chapter 5.

The citing of qualifications by only 20 per cent of interviewees also needs to be seen in the light of the fact, as we saw in Chapter 2, that 96 per cent of interviewees hold higher education qualifications, with a substantial number holding post-graduate awards as well. Here again, it appears likely that they view qualifications as a necessary, but not sufficient, cause of their success. The other factors mentioned also understate, often dramatically, the importance actually represented by them in our interviewees' lives. While only 6 per cent explicitly cite mentoring as a major factor in their success, for instance, 44 per cent of our interviewees mention mentors who have been important to them in their careers.

Moreover, while only one interviewee explicitly mentions image as a major factor in success, a substantial number comment at other stages of their interviews on the importance which they personally place on their appearance and image. All but two interviewees were very well dressed, and a number admit that they spend significant amounts of money on their appearance:

Image is absolutely crucial. The secret of success is performance, image and exposure. Very often the performance content makes up no more than 10 per cent. I've visited a colour consultant and have now changed my whole dress and colour sense. Now I look in the mirror and I like what I see. It's given me immeasurable confidence in myself, which I otherwise lacked. I feel no guilt in spending two or three hundred pounds on a dress for work.

I spend quite a lot of money on elegant, classic clothes.

Image is very important. I spent large sums of money on my wardrobe.

There are also frank assessments of other kinds of reasons for success:

I've tried to make the system work for me. I've been helped by the fact that [my field] is not seen as at as high a level as [others]. I would probably have found it much more difficult to reach the level I have in other areas.

The most successful women I know nearly all have a streak of ruthlessness about them. It's not that they will trample over everyone else and over all other considerations to get what they want — most of them won't. It's rather that they have a clear view of what they want and where they are going, and they are usually prepared to pay the price needed to achieve it.

Overall, however, there is an apparent contrast between the factors specifically cited by our interviewees when they were asked about the reasons for their success and the factors which appear to emerge from analysis of the rest of the interview material. As we shall see in the next chapter, the management styles of our interviewees are based on long-term strategic thinking, making choices based on a shrewd assessment of the options, fostering teamwork, and maintaining a high degree of commitment to the goals of their organisations. Scase and Goffee (1989) suggest that both male and female managers tend to cite such characteristics as important for career success in general. Many of our interviewees, however, appear to feel a certain gap between themselves and the fact that they are clearly successful in their present or most immediate past employment. In some ways, it seems as if they are alienated from their own success. It is a phenomenon which we shall consider further in Chapter 6.

Emerging patterns

As we suggested at the beginning of this chapter, our interviewees' career patterns appear to have more in common with one another than with those of their male counterparts. The dominant features of the pattern include moves amongst a number of apparently disparate occupations, changes of employer every four to seven years, and relatively late achievement of recognised senior positions. Constantly present, as the background on which these tapestried careers are stitched, is the gender factor in individuals' private and public lives.

FACTORS IN CAREER DEVELOPMENT

While some of the major factors in our interviewees' career development relate to specific professional and managerial posts, many other important factors are a direct or indirect outcome of their domestic lives. Both the professional and the domestic factors appear to have had apparently contradictory effects: they have reinforced interviewees' personal qualities, thereby strengthening their career prospects, at the same time as they have constrained the pursuit of professional success.

The three most important factors which appear to be implicated in our interviewees' professional success are the acquisition of a very high level of educational qualifications, the transference of skills from one occupation to another and a pronounced impetus towards growth and development.

As we have already noted, 96 per cent of our interviewees hold higher education qualifications. In many cases, their array of degrees, diplomas and certificates exceeds the normal entry standard for particular professions. In this respect, our interviewees could be seen as implementing the belief of female managers that women require more qualifications then men to reach the same levels in management (SIACE, 1990). Moreover, as we shall see in Chapter 6, it is in this very area of achieving qualifications that most of our interviewees recommend younger women to follow in their footsteps.

But what has been the effect in practice of their being so highly qualified? Their extensive experimentation after completing their initial full-time education means that many of them now work in posts for which their initial qualifications may be both unnecessary and, even, appear slightly odd: thus, a physics graduate now works in academic marketing; a number of holders of law degrees work in entirely non-legal jobs while a qualified secretary works in law; a chemistry graduate now works in accountancy. Such divergence from the subject matter of the first degree is, of course, found in many graduates of both sexes, but we suspect that it may be somewhat more pronounced for our interviewees than it would be for their male professional peers.

When we consider the way in which our interviewees have become so highly qualified, there is unquestionably at least one other major difference between them and their male professional peers. Uncharacteristically for Scottish professionals as a whole there are substantial numbers of mature students amongst our interviewees. Our interviewees who were mature students fit into the pattern whereby female mature students in higher education tend to pay for themselves, whereas their male counterparts tend to a significantly greater extent to have fees paid by their employers (see, for instance, Nelson, 1989; Munn and MacDonald, 1988). On the whole, then, those of our interviewees who acquired their higher education qualifications as mature students did so under particularly demanding circumstances. As one of them reports:

> I returned to [university] to read law over two years, self-financed . . . I temped in secretarial work during the holidays. I worked solidly for two years with one night a week free.

A second major factor in our interviewees' career development appears to have been the extent to which they carried over skills from one occupation to another. Indeed, one of their most typical career moves is being seconded to new projects, which lead to new skills and contacts which then provide the basis for the next major move. Our interviewees are also often conscious of the similarities between apparently disparate fields of work: 'the construction industry is similar to the health service in many ways — in both you must adapt projects to the needs of the client' says one interviewee who has worked in both fields.

Equally typical is the experience of the woman whose experiential learning in a voluntary organisation proves invaluable in her next professional or managerial appointment. A number of our interviewees moved from running voluntary organisations as volunteers to running small businesses or departments. The effects of transferring skills are not always wholly congenial, however: 'you run our home as if it were an office' complained one interviewee's daughter to her mother.

Our interviewees' working lives are also characterised by growth. Many of them undertook jobs which then grew under them or for which they had seen a lack in their particular company. One interviewee for instance, reports:

> I saw that there was no marketing department in [my company] so I wrote out a marketing plan and gave it to one of the directors. My ideas, much to my astonishment, were accepted. So I helped to set up the group marketing section of which I am now in charge.

Moreover, despite the general lack of progression from part-time to analogous full-time jobs, a few of our interviewees did move from lecturing part-time to lecturing full-time in their chosen academic field. Counting both such expansion from part-time to full-time as well as the often dramatic growth in job specifications, there is a noticeable trend amongst our interviewees to increase their professional responsibilities in ways other than by standard promotions.

Together with these factors which appear positively to have strengthened our interviewees' career development, there is evidence about the constraining factors which they have also experienced. The most prominent of these constraints are those associated with domestic expectations.

The issue of geographical mobility is a major one for a substantial number of our interviewees. In most cases interviewees have felt commitments to partners who had, or were unwilling, to move. In what appears to be a growing trend, there are a number of dual site marriages as representing perhaps the only equitable solution for dual career couples. In other cases, there is clear evidence that a considerable number of our interviewees have foregone advantageous career moves in order to continue to live with a partner.

The demands of child and of parent care will be considered in much greater detail in Chapter 5. For now it is worth noting that, regardless of the extent to which child and parent care arrangements may have constrained the short-term career development of our interviewees, such constraints do not appear to have affected their careers overall. In the longer term, the few years during which many women took either full or partial career breaks seem to have postponed their major professional achievements until only a few years later than their female colleagues.

Other than those related to mobility and child care, we have not considered in this chapter any of the many career development issues connected with our interviewees' relationships with their partners; that analysis appears in Chapter 5. It might be worth noting here, however, that one major factor in many interviewees' career considerations is the attitude of their spouse or partner. Our interviewees report a significant number of instances in which the domestic and career expectations of their partner have directly conflicted with their own.

As well as factors that both strengthened and constrained the career development of our interviewees, their own personal characteristics have also clearly played an important role in shaping their professional successes. We shall examine in Chapter 4 those of their characteristics which they believe are important in their working relationships with colleagues. For now we should like to consider briefly some of the characteristics which our interviewees appear to share with each other and which appear to have an effect on their long-term career development.

PERSONAL CHARACTERISTICS

The major characteristics of most of our interviewees as children appear to have played an important role in the later careers: their early eagerness to assume responsibility, their excellence in performance, their organising abilities, and their commitment to causes they believe in, all feature largely in their adult lives. And, as they did when they were children, they continue to view their success as largely a matter of luck.

But, during the course of their lives as professionals and managers, nearly all of our interviewees acknowledge the effects of gender on the shape of their careers. Most of them have come to believe that substantial barriers are placed in the way of women, barriers which are erected both by men and by women themselves.

Rather than protesting to men or trying to change other women, our interviewees on the whole choose to act positively to overcome the obstacles. They work extremely hard at the professional activities and at the ways in which they present themselves in public. They are almost invincibly determined: after completing her post-graduate training, one interviewee worked at a long series of part-time temporary jobs until there was a rare vacancy in the field in which she wanted to make her career; another continued over several years to apply for senior posts despite feeling that she was 'always the bridesmaid, never the groom'.

Conscious of the need continually to prove that they are at least as good as, and usually better than, their male colleagues, our interviewees refuse to protest about such assumptions. Instead, they proceed to prove themselves, as one of them explicitly recounts:

> [One post] was a very hard job. I had to prove myself, because only one woman had worked there before. I proved myself to my male colleagues by [succeeding in a particularly difficult task], then my life became a lot easier. But even now it annoys me that I had to prove myself before I was accepted.'

CREATING CAREERS

The result of these factors and personal characteristics is the creation of what we are calling career tapestries. Both the overall design and the weaving are complex, and it is often hard to see what might link the apparently disparate elements together. But overall a sense of coherence of purpose prevails, and interviewees' career moves turn out to be more integrated than at first appears. For instance, our interviewees show a pronounced tendency to make career moves where one, often minor element in an earlier post becomes the predominant pattern of the next. Thus, an interviewee, who had worked in careers guidance, developed a deep commitment to careers guidance for adults and eventually moved into continuing education. A teacher who had committed herself to working with her trade union fund that the insight she gained became an essential part of her work in local government. A researcher developed her interest in one highly specific scientific field into a broader concern for the social responsibility of science.

It is true that fortuitous elements remain in the public lives of our interviewees — much as one might find unexplained strange creatures in a seventeenth-century tapestry. Thus, a number of interviewees have moved to posts because on previous chance encounters they had deeply impressed senior managers with their ability. Broadly speaking, however, the strong impression which our interviewees leave about their career patterns is that of women who are very much in charge of their own lives, and who enjoy the experience of creating their own patterns.

Chapter Four

Women as Leaders

Introduction

In Chapter 3, we tried to identify the emergent patterns in the factors which appear to have shaped the professional careers of our interviewees. We should now like to try to turn to those qualities — the skills, attributes and experience, as a job specification might phrase them — which characterise our interviewees' successful professional and managerial lives.

We shall first consider interviewees' attitudes towards their work, their perceptions of their management styles and the extent to which they believe that management training — or the lack of it — has helped to shape their way of working. We shall then discuss the interaction of gender with management or professional style. Here we shall look at how far our interviewees believe that theirs is a specifically female style and how far male attitudes appear to have shaped their ways of working; nearly all of our interviewees work predominantly with male peers, report to more senior male staff, and have responsibility for both male and female staff. Finally, we shall propose a model of those qualities which appear to characterise our interviewees' style of leadership.

Attitudes towards work

Watson (1989) found that all but one of her well known and successful interviewees experience a lack of joy in their careers; on the whole, they do not enjoy their work. Our overall findings are the reverse. All of our interviewees express enthusiasm for their work; nearly all think that they are good at what they do and many express a deeply felt commitment to the goals of their organisation and a sense of fulfilment in helping to meet those aims.

Chapter 3 has already noted our interviewees' widespread sense of commitment to work. What also comes through strongly in our interviews is sheer pleasure in work. Typical comments include:

> I've greatly enjoyed my career to date. (Education)

> I enjoy my work. There is a great deal of flexibility in it and I value the freedom of the job. It's also extremely varied. (Voluntary organisation)

> I thrive on my job. I thoroughly enjoy meeting and talking to new people. (Government)

> I get a great deal of pleasure from nearly all of the work that I do — even the apparently mundane tasks — because I can see how it helps to bring about the kinds of changes I believe in. I'm extremely lucky in that most of the work is also enjoyable for its own sake — meeting congenial people, travelling throughout the world, reading widely, and solving problems that are just complex enough to be challenging but rarely present insuperable difficulties. (Voluntary organisation)

As we have noted in Chapter 3, a number of our interviewees also feel particularly fortunate because their husbands' income leaves them financially free to choose whether or not to work outside their homes in the first place. They believe, in other words, that they have chosen freely to work. The overwhelming impression, both from those who choose to work as well as from those who have to support themselves and sometimes their family, is that their work represents a bedrock of their identity and that they feel fulfilled through it — as well as in other ways. The management styles with which they identify themselves thus often appear to be deeply personal.

Perceptions of management style

Because of the rarity of senior women in Scotland, it is difficult to disentangle the various sources and elements of their management styles. Which characteristics relate specifically to their being female? Which styles are simply those appropriate to their chosen profession? The problem is particularly acute because the majority of our interviewees believe that women do tend to manage differently from men. Nevertheless, in what follows we have tried first to identify the general characteristics of our interviewees as managers before proceeding to an analysis of what they perceive as the effects of gender.

We have already noted in Chapter 2 the strong organisational flair of our interviewees as children. We were thus not suprised to hear a considerable number of our interviewees speak of the importance of long-term strategic thinking both for their organisations as a whole and for their own responsibilities within their workplaces:

> I try always to keep in front of me an idea of where I want [my organisation] to be in five years' time, and most of my major decisions are made in the context of a long-term strategic plan. (Voluntary organisation)

A second major characteristic of management styles as our interviewees identify them is flexibility of approach — taking different tactics depending on context and purpose and being highly selective about which issues to confront:

> I wish to be liked, and this often works. But sometimes it's better to be disliked, to stand up and be counted. But it's stressful to be confrontational, and I only do it sometimes — with effect — on a few selected issues. I'm less confrontational now on issues of gendered language. [My own profession] and females in [my own institution] are issues that I will fight on. (Education)

A third major characteristic is that of challenging methods and ideas which they feel to be suspect:

> One of my aims has been to demystify [education] and to enable change. I have always been one to challenge sacred cows. (Education)

> I've never been afraid to speak my mind and to challenge things I didn't like. (Government)

> I am almost ashamed to say how much I enjoy challenging ideas and practices which I find unjustifiable or of poor quality. (Voluntary organisation)

A fourth characteristic is concern for firm action combined with fairness:

> I think I'm a good manager. I'm certainly not soft . . . I have a good working relationship with my staff, I feel, but you'd really have to ask them what they thought of me! (Industry)

> I have a very strong organisational sense. I'm not afraid to take disciplinary

action against colleagues or to make decisions which are hard ones. It's important to act as a leader, to be fair, to be seen not to be showing favour, to be approachable but not too approachable. (Government)

I feel strongly about being fair and being seen to be fair. It's one reason why I distrust the informal procedures that often seem to prevail in a small country like Scotland: when you don't have to account for your procedures and decisions in an explicit way, you can too easily use criteria for making decisions that might not be acceptable if they were spelled out. I don't believe in unfettered democracy — no organisation could ever be effectively run on that basis — but I do believe in explicit accountability for methods and procedures as well as for goals. (Voluntary organisation)

A preference for working as a team, consulting and communicating, is a fifth major characteristic:

I'm a good listener. I like my staff to be self-motivating. I'm very keen on building up a staff team. (Finance)

I have a laissez-faire attitude towards management. I expect people to do their work. But I am very keen on developing a team spirit. Departmental meetings are crucial. (Health)

The key to good management is a good communications system. (Voluntary organisation)

How are such characteristics of what our interviewees see as good management acquired? How far does training help? As we shall see next, although our interviewees hold apparently diverse views on these questions, some trends do emerge.

Perceived Need for Training

The need for improving the quality and quantity of management training for both men and women is now widely recognised in principle in Scotland as a whole: SIACE (1990), for instance, shows that 85 per cent of employers say that their organisation encourages women to train and develop for management positions. The practice, however, appears to lag somewhat behind the theory: only 43 per cent of women managers in Scotland say that they have received management training for their present jobs (ibid). Handy (1987) has also found that, comparatively, British employers are reluctant to invest in management education and training for either men or women.

How do our interviewees fit into this pattern? We cannot say with any degree of statistical certainty. Because the interviews were semi-structured and several of them unavoidably cut short, our data cover the formal management training — or the lack of it — for only twenty-nine of our interviewees. However, because these twenty-nine are spread across the full age range and nearly the full areas of work of our interviewees (the exception is the media), the responses which we do have may be at least indicative of trends in attitudes towards management training.

Of the twenty-nine interviewees for whom we have information about management training, nine have received no management training. Six of these nine interviewees, who cover a wide professional spread but who tend to be either relatively young or near to retirement, are sceptical about the value of management training:

> I wonder about the value of theoretical training for management. Perhaps a commonsense approach is better — to treat people the way you would want to be treated yourself. (Industry)

> I have not had any formal management training but feel that I manage a great deal better than my predecessor. (Finance)

> I have not had any formal management training but I don't see that as a great disadvantage. The person at the top should be as much a leader as a manager. (Education)

The other three without training recognise its potential value:

> I am a gardener rather than a disciplinarian. This could be a problem if I had responsibility for a large number of staff and I would then seek training for it. I've never had any management training. I have not felt the need to date, but it would be extremely useful if I were moving to new fields. I would buy it for myself if necessary. (Education)

> I have never had any formal management training, but at some stage I want to undertake it. (Voluntary organisation)

By contrast, nearly 70 per cent of those interviewees for whom we have such information have undertaken management training. Such training tends to be at the level of a Masters of Business Administration, but it also includes short courses both certificated and non-certificated. Regardless of the type of course, our interviewees report that the results have invariably been useful:

> I thought I was quite a good manager. I greatly appreciated having studied for a diploma in management studies which gave me the theory which I was then able to put into practice. (Government)

I've studied for a higher national certificate in management studies over two years in the evenings. It did help. I've also done an Open University Managing Organisations course, and I'm now considering doing an MBA. I've also learned a great deal on the job. I've certainly learned to be a lot more patient and to get what I want by a more roundabout than by a direct approach. (Voluntary organisation)

I've taken an Open University effective managers course, which I found very helpful. (Education)

I am highly committed to the training of all levels of staff both to do their present jobs better and to move to better jobs. I try to put into practice what I believe for myself as well. I've been on a number of management training courses and am about to start an MBA with the Open University. I've found almost all of the training very relevant to my job; most of it was also thoroughly enjoyable! (Voluntary organisation)

It is likely that this emphasis on training — for themselves and for their staff — is closely related to the fact, as we noted in Chapter 2, that 96 per cent of our interviewees hold higher education qualifications; to a certain extent our interviewees merely illustrate the fact that those who have more education seek still more education and training (Munn and MacDonald, 1988). There is some evidence to suggest, however, that gender issues are also implicated. A substantial number of interviewees refer spontaneously to what they see as the specific need to train women for management, in order to overcome the restrictive effects of both male and female attitudes towards women:

Discrimination still exists in most institutions. It's difficult to know how to break it down. I was greatly helped by a course I attended on interpersonal skills run by the Pepperell Unit. (Education)

I was seen as an extremely good executive secretary, and that infuriated me. So I looked around at what else I might do and thought of studying for an MBA. (Industry)

I have at times had doubts about my own confidence and abilities. I'm very keen on assertiveness and confidence-building courses for women. (Finance)

I'm a bit ambivalent about women. To a certain extent they are their own worst enemies. They're often too hesitant. Training is crucial. (Education)

The very high value placed by some of our interviewees on obtaining a managerial qualification means that they see one as so essential that they are willing to make substantial sacrifices for it:

I'm currently studying for an MBA. This, and the demands of my job, don't leave me with much time for social life. But I feel that gaining the MBA is crucial to my future career advancement and therefore more important than my social life. (Finance)

I'm seriously considering taking an MBA with the Open University, although I know it will place a great strain on my life at home and on my spare time. But I want to do it to underpin my practical skills with a more theoretical understanding and, frankly, to improve my prospects for promotion in the future. (Education)

In this intense commitment to obtaining managerial qualifications, our interviewees appear to have much in common with the 53 per cent of women managers in Scotland (as differentiated from only 20 per cent of employers) who believe that women require more qualifications than men to reach the same levels in management (SIACE, 1990). How far do such perceptions reflect the reality of life at work for women in senior positions? We shall try to suggest answers in the section which follows.

Gender at Work: Male Attitudes

The realities of working life for most of our interviewees include working with both men and women, typically in a hierarchy in which those to whom they report and their peers are predominantly or entirely males, while those for whom they are directly responsible include both males and females. The extent of reporting upwards, and of direct responsibility for other workers varies substantially amongst our interviewees. A principal or director of an institution has substantial managerial responsibility, while a head of department in a large organisation may have less autonomy; in turn, professionals such as advocates or journalists may have few workers for whom they have direct managerial responsibility.

As we have seen in Chapter 3, most of our interviewees believe that gender has been an important factor in shaping their career paths as far as their appointment to new posts is concerned: decisions about children, questions about partners' geographical mobility, outright and subtle sex discrimination, informal male networking, and both male and female restrictive attitudes towards women are all seen as helping to shape particular career paths. But what happens in the workplace itself? How far does being a woman appear to affect our interviewees' professional experiences?

In the first place, nearly all of our interviewees believe that many, or even most, men experience difficulties in working with women as their peers or their leaders. These difficulties take many subtle and varied forms. Informal male networking, including direct exclusion of women through homosexuality, is one factor:

> Meetings are handled autocratically. Things are decided beforehand in the staff club, with informal male networking. There is also quite a large element of homosexuality which excludes women. At times I have found that my presence was very threatening; I might as well have been from outer space. (Education)

Male preferences for working with other males is also noted:

> Men fall into two categories: chauvinists — and lots of men don't like working with women — and a few very supportive ones. Men are quite often frightened of women, especially if they are intelligent women. Men like being in herds; they like everyone being the same. This often causes problems if a woman suddenly comes on the scene. (Industry)

> Very often men are either suspicious of women or contemptuous of them. Many men find it difficult to relate to a female boss. (Education)

> Most men would prefer to work with other men. They believe that a small percentage of women are very good, but that the rest are emotional, illogical and a bloody nuisance. (Industry)

> Some men just don't know how to work with female colleagues. (Education)

Men's unwarranted assumptions about female interests also emerge as a source of annoyance:

> I sometimes get annoyed that I'm not included in certain work projects, especially ones that are engineering oriented, because of my gender. 'We didn't think we'd ask you because we didn't think you'd be interested in it'. (Industry)

Men's active hostility to women in senior positions is implicit in several of these comments and is explicitly described by other interviewees:

> I've developed a skin as thick as a rhino; therefore being a female is not a great disadvantage. But it hasn't helped particularly either, and I have faced a certain hostility in the firm. I've heard one comment about me as 'this trumped up woman; she must think she's a proper manager; she must be after a car!' When problems with any of my staff occur, I hear the statement 'What can you expect? Two women can't work together.' I know my department is called 'The Bimbettes' and that sometimes I'm referred to as the Jezebel of the company. (Industry)

Laurie Taylor

The first meeting of a brand new association of university professors will take place in London on Saturday, March 4.

Rather a good sherry, don't you think?
Very fine.

Not a bad turnout. Especially with all that bad weather in the north.
Most promising.

And rather a nice atmosphere.
Relaxed.

Yes, indeed.
But then there's something rather reassuring about being in such a large group of professors.

Among one's own kind.
People who appreciate one's point of view.

That's it. None of that usual whingeing about promotion prospects from top-of-the scale lecturers.

None of those malicious assertions from jealous colleagues that by today's standards most of us would be lucky to get a short-term contract.

Quite. And none of that silly nonsense about us making the most of our administration so there isn't a second left over to do any teaching.
That's right. And none of those bully-boy AUT types trying to stop one carrying out one's professional duties.

And none of those management-mad people from the admin block telling one how to run one's department.
Oh yes. And none of those cocky new blood appointments who think they own the earth simply because they have a few thousand pounds worth of research money.

And none of those busy-body vice chancellors with lower-seconds in engineering.
And none of those – erm – how can I put it?

Yes?
None of those – you know – medium height . . .

Yes, go on
Erm . . . soft-spoken . . .
Erm . . .

Yes?
Clean-shaven . . . Erm

None of those *women*?
That's it! Refill for you?

Splendid.

I've recently been at a dinner . . . at which I'd been one of the very few females, and, in fact, was the only female at my table. I talked with colleagues about a range of different matters, none linked to [our common professional concern]. Afterwards it was reported that one of the men at the table had commented to another, 'She's a most attractive woman but probably a hard bitch to get money out of'. (Finance)

When I was first appointed, I was encouraged to take a teacher training course and did. It caused quite a lot of jealousy when I shone on the course and got three credits. I was the only female on the course, and there were many comments from my male friends. (Education)

In the eyes of our interviewees, gender seems rarely to be acknowledged as an issue in institutions which have traditionally been dominated by males:

I'm the only person in [my department] who sees gender at work as an issue. For demographic trends reasons it has become slightly fashionable to look at it but . . . there is no theoretical base beneath that. I only really became a feminist when I came to work in [my institution] . . . I just found it such a male-dominated establishment. It just absolutely amazed me. I never thought that I would be coming to that. I always thought that the academic life was a life based on egalitarianism, and it's not . . . People still can't see it as strange that there are virtually no females on any [institutional] committees, even new ones. (Education)

I was recently speaking to [a senior manager] who was particularly pleased about the fact that he had recently appointed a number of women to senior positions. But I was startled to learn that he did not believe that their gender would be likely to have any effect either on them or on their male colleagues, most of whom had never worked with women in senior roles before. So, of course, he saw no need for monitoring the situation, supporting the woman or helping their male colleagues to learn new ways of working. (Voluntary organisation)

But the difficulties in men and women working together, many of our interviewees believe, also stem from women themselves:

Men find it difficult to relate to women, to criticise women's work. Women often don't like being criticised, perhaps because they get too involved in their work. (Government)

It is then perhaps not surprising that, in turn, a number of our interviewees express active dislike of the world of males at work:

I have no great admiration for men. In fact, I like women a great deal more than I like men. Men often take the credit for women's work. (Media)

> I don't really like the man's world. (Education)

Such comments are almost equally balanced, however, by others suggesting that the male world has been fully accepted and internalised:

> I take it as a compliment if I am sitting in a committee, and the chairman refers to the members as gentlemen. It shows that I've been fully accepted by the group rather than being an outsider. (Education)

Overall, although our interviewees recognise the difficulties in working with men, they tend simply to acknowledge the problems and then get on with their professional concerns. In particular, they tend to treat sexual harassment as a comparatively trivial matter, as we shall see below. Many of them believe that the next generation will be easier to work with:

> Organisations vary enormously in their attitude towards women. Hurdles do exist. I think it's a generational thing. Attitudes are changing, especially amongst younger men. (Government)

Most of our interviewees actively prefer working with men, or with both men and women, rather than working primarily with other women:

> I prefer mixed networks of fellow professionals. Many of the problems identified by the women's movement face men as well as women. It's really time to look at both genders. (Education)

> I like working with both men and women rather than with only women or only men. I especially enjoy bringing together a range of strengths and skills into a coherent strategy, and find this easiest to do in mixed sex groups. (Voluntary organisation)

> I prefer working in a social environment with men in it rather than with all female groups. (Government)

> At the end of the day I prefer working with men. (Education)

We shall return in Chapter 6 and the Conclusion to this matter of women and men working together. Meanwhile, let us look briefly at another gender-related subject which is often believed to be particularly detrimental to women at work — sexual harassment.

Gender at work: sexual harassment

The existence of sexual harassment at work is a subject which unites most of our interviewees: 81 per cent of those who directly replied to a question about sexual discrimination and harassment believe that both exist in their own or other women's professional lives. At first nearly all of our interviewees said that they personally have not experienced sexual harassment. When this response was probed, a number reported receiving patronising remarks or being ignored at meetings. But few take it very seriously in their present positions. 'They wouldn't dare sexually harass me,' is a fairly frequent response.

In the past, as more junior employees, however, a number have experienced sexual harassment and have dealt with it explicitly and openly:

> For a while I worked for a medical publisher as personal assistant to the managing director. This was the first time that I had to deal with sexism — I was told by my boss that I was on a good salary for a woman — and I dealt with it by public rebuke. It never happened again. (Voluntary organisation)

> When I was nineteen or twenty I was in [an organisation] where the . . . manager would quite deliberately brush against you when walking in and out to [where he worked]. All the female office staff experienced it, but I was the only one who was prepared to speak up. I just asked him one day if he would stop it, and he did. Unfortunately, about a week later, I was called into head office and moved from that branch to a different one. At the time I slightly regretted speaking out and wondered whether it would affect my career, but I now think I did the right thing and I am glad. (Finance)

> As an apprentice journalist, I once had to interview a cinema manager about what was showing for the following week. The interview took place in a very small, dark room. The cinema manager's hands wandered from time to time. I eventually managed to persuade my editor that someone else should write that column and opted out of the situation. Sexual harassment I now feel is something that tends to happen to young girls . . . . often immature girls . . . It is wrong, and it should be stopped. (Media)

> I've very occasionally suffered from sexual harassment. I was once propositioned by a stockbroker at a residential event. But I feel that I can cope with such approaches. (Finance)

There is general agreement that, while sexual harassment represents a problem for more junior women, women in senior posts can afford simply to ignore it or to treat it humorously:

> Probably the best way of dealing with sexual harassment of a minor kind is ignoring it. (Media)

> Sexual harassment such as pats on the shoulder and being called 'my dear' are usually best ignored or laughed at. (Finance)

I've experienced sexual harassment only in small ways — dears, darlings, pats on the shoulder. It sometimes annoys me, but I can cope with it fairly easily. (Industry)

I've suffered from time to time from patronising remarks; usually humour is the best way to deal with them. (Finance)

Our interviewees' reluctance to pursue issues of sexual harassment, as with their reluctance to pursue cases of sexual discrimination, has, of course, a solid basis in the experience of the real world of employment. As Corcoran (1988) shows:

There are real and practical dangers in making a complaint of discrimination . . . The complainant may be regarded as a troublemaker and not be offered jobs or promotion in the future. Her work may be scrutinised more often or more carefully than before. She may be moved to less satisfying or lower paid work. Where reorganisation results in redundancy, she may be the one the employer chooses to dismiss.

On the whole, however, our interviewees appear to feel so comfortable in their predominatly male worlds, that issues such as sexual harassment become minor irritants rather than major issues. But what of their attitudes towards the other women with whom they work? How far do they feel any sense of kindred with them?

Gender at work: do women support other women?

Many of our interviewees express a feeling that, as women, they have an obligation to help other women in their organisations:

I feel responsible for young women in [my organisation] and try, as best I can, to bring them forward. (Voluntary organisation)

During my present job I have introduced a number of equal opportunities developments to [local government], including a paper on job sharing. I don't support positive discrimination, but I am sympathetic to the special needs of women. (Government)

I've tried to be very encouraging to other female staff; I think of myself as a gardening boss. I have been, and have sent some of my staff, on Pepperell Unit courses. (Finance)

I try actively to mentor both men and women whom I see as especially able and capable of career development. My own priorities at work have

emphasised equal opportunities in gender to a greater extent than I should
ideally have preferred, simply because it seems to me that women in
Scotland start from much further behind than almost anywhere in the
developed world. (Education)

I have developed an equal opportunities statement for [my organisation].
(Voluntary organisation)

I am very aware of gender as an issue in management. Equal opportunities
policies are crucial. (Industry)

In this positive awareness of equal opportunities for both sexes, our
interviewees share the attitudes of many employers in Scotland: 77 per
cent of employers believe that 'senior managers need to put women
forward for more training and education', while 57.5 per cent say that
their organisation has a written equal opportunities policy and 80 per cent
rate their organisation's response to equal opportunities as good. 87 per
cent of employers agree that 'everyone needs training in equal
opportunities' (SIACE, 1990).

How far such expressions of policy are effective in practice is, of course,
a more complex matter. SIACE (1990) has found that female employees
take a very different view from their predominantly male employers about
the effectiveness of such policies: only 27 per cent of female aspirant
managers disagree with the statement 'our equal opportunities policy is
only there for show', as differentiated from 80.5 per cent of employers.
Because of the range of the interview questions and because we did not
speak to their staff, it is not possible to assess how far the equal
opportunities in gender policies adopted by most of our interviewees are
actually effective in practice. At the very crude level of the choice of their
successors, however, it is interesting to note that when at least three of
our interviewees have moved to new posts between the time of interview
and our writing this book, other women have been appointed to fill their
positions.

The attitude of responsibility towards other women which is expressed
by our interviewees appears even more generous when we consider the
fact that such advocacy can often be dangerous for women attempting to
succeed on male terms. Vallance (1988), for instance, notes that women
politicians who do not mention women's interests at all do better than
those who do. She argues that women are labelled, in exactly the way in
which many of them fear, for showing even a modicum of sustained
interest in the rights and concerns of their own sex. One of our
interviewees speaks frankly about the dilemma:

Interestingly enough, I've just been discussing this matter [of responsibility

for other women] with my mentor. Although she also is a strong supporter
of equal opportunities, she advised me against trying to promote such issues
until I had been in any job for at least three or four years. In her view, trying
to act as an advocate for women at too early a stage would result in
ineffectiveness as far as other women were concerned and stagnation in my
own career. (Education)

In this context, several of out interviewees emphasise the fact that the
present, almost equal, gender balance of their staff has arisen by chance
rather than by deliberate choice or policy. One interviewee is explicitly
unsympathetic to the problems of her female staff:

I don't like women bringing their domestic problems to work. I don't do it,
and I don't expect anyone else to do so. (Finance)

Such an attitude is rarely expressed by other interviewees, despite the fact
that a number of them believe that women are often primarily responsible
for their own under-representation in senior positions.

Overall, however, our interviewees appear to be committed to the need
for preparing and implementing equal opportunities policies. Does this
heightened awareness of gender as an issue to be addressed at work extend
to their own assessment of themselves as female managers? How far do
they believe that a female management style exists? And how far do they
assess their own management styles as specifically female?

Gender at work: is there a female management style?

Much of the now extensive literature on women in management tends
cither to assume or to show that there are 'male' and 'female' styles of
management (see, for example, Baines, 1988; Marshall, 1984; Scase and
Goffee, 1989; Coyle and Skinner, 1988), although neither style is
practised exclusively by one sex. The qualities often associated with
'male' styles include competitiveness, preference for hierarchial
structures, liking for bureaucratic procedures and conformity. Those
most often associated with 'female' styles include co-operation and
seeking consensus, preference for supportive structures, flexibility and the
ability to learn from readily admitted mistakes. Increasingly, companies
and other organisations are seeking deliberately to encourage their
manager to use both 'male' and 'female' styles (BBC, 1990), with both
men and women selecting their styles according to the context and
purpose of the work for which they are responsible.

How far is this development reflected in our interviewees? Of the
thirty-eight interviewees who gave definite responses to the question

about gendered management styles, 58 per cent believe that there are 'female' styles of management, while 39 per cent disagree (the other interviewee for whom we have this data is uncertain). Even for those who disagree that they have a specifically 'female' management style, however, at least some of the characteristics of their own style as they report it tend to cluster at the 'female' end of the spectrum of characteristics:

> People tend to assess management style by gender, but personality is probably a lot more important. I myself have a fairly informal management style, and a fairly unconventional one. This can work for or against you. But I hope that mainly it's an advantage. A lot of management is just common sense. (Government)

> My own style as a manager emphasises co-operation, team-building, sharing of good ideas, flexibility. I'm always looking out for innovation and new development. I sometimes find it unpleasant to discipline staff, but I am always ready to assume responsibility. (Voluntary organisation)

> My management style is different from others around me, but I'm not sure if this is because I have worked in a number of different environments or because I am a woman. The fact that I am more sympathetic and talk more to people may possibly be because of the American influence. (Industry)

One interviewee is emphatic in rejecting any idea of herself as a female leader:

> We need to stop thinking about women and to start thinking about people . . . I would not like to be classed first and foremost as female but more as a successful business person. (Industry)

Several other cite traits in themselves which are traditionally associated with males:

> I am very often called a hard woman, but I see myself as determined! (Finance)

> I am a driver, but that's more to do with personality than with gender. I've been called an autocrat. (Government)

> I have been called ruthless and bloody-minded. (Industry)

> I don't mind if I'm regarded as being aggressive. (Finance)

Overall, most of our interviewees across all sectors associate themselves to some extent with what they see as 'female' management styles. Their style is characterised, most notably, by an emphasis on inclusive, co-operative ways of working:

> I manage differently because I am a woman. Women manage in a more democratic way rather than using the power game and politics that men often do. (Industry)

> I do work differently from men. Men can be much more confrontational. (Voluntary organisation)

> My own management style is very participative. (Education)

> I do manage differently from all the other directors, who are, incidentally, male. I try to delegate to other people and then try not to interfere. I don't hold meetings automatically, as many of my fellow directors do. And I try to give credit for the work of my staff, which many other directors I know probably claim for themselves. (Industry)

> My management style is definitely different from that of a man. I am much more consultative, caring and non-confrontational. (Education)

> Women who have different styles of management. I'm very involved in bringing my staff together to work as part of a team. I don't care who comes up with the good ideas. I'm certainly not afraid to make decisions. (Finance)

As the last comment suggests, co-operative styles are not seen as a form of weakness or of indecisiveness, but rather as one important kind of strength. As one interviewee points out:

> Women often have a more intimate, caring management style, but we're quite capable of doing all the hard-edged bits as well. (Law)

Another major strength which emerges from our interviewees' responses is that of dealing with real or underlying problems by rooting them out and tackling them directly:

> I'm a hard worker and always must get to the bottom of problems. If not, we just stack up more problems. (Finance)

> Women are more pro-active. They don't leave problems festering to the same extent as men. (Government)

> I always say what I think. Men don't. Men often tell their boss what they want to hear rather than the truth. (Finance)

A third major area of strength in a 'female' management style appears in our interviewees' comments about what they see as women's lack of ego and willingness to admit mistakes:

> You treat yourself less seriously if you're a woman. Men probably think they deserve to be managers. (Voluntary organisation)

> Women are a lot less pompous than men. (Finance)

> Women are very task oriented and usually have less ego than men. They're more willing to negotiate and more willing to admit difficulties. (Education)

> You often learn more from doing things wrong than by doing them right. (Voluntary organisation)

Fourthly, our interviewees mention a range of skills which have traditionally been associated with home management and the demands of child rearing:

> Women are especially good at time management and multi-tasking. (Industry)

> Women generally have a sense of caring about their job and put a great deal of energy into it. (Government)

> Women do tend to manage differently from men — they are usually much more flexible. (Finance)

But our interviewees do not see all female management traits as necessarily helpful:

> Women managers do work differently. They take other people's feelings into account. This can be a help and a hindrance. (Voluntary organisation)

> I don't know if I am a good manager. I am good at planning but I find it difficult to . . . cope with lying and dishonesty. I simply can't accept that other people might cheat. But they do, and I always fail to make allowances for it. (Education)

Many of the characteristics of management style in general which our interviewees mention, but which they do not identify specifically as 'female', also tend to cluster around the 'female' end of the spectrum of management style: the characteristics, noted earlier in this chapter, of flexibility, challenging accepted practice, consulting and communicating, are all ones mentioned by some of our interviewees as being 'female'. But

Our interviewees tend to believe that, in the end, the problems faced by managers are human, rather than gendered, issues:

> Issues can appear to be women's issues, but very often they are human issues. (Voluntary organisation)

There is some evidence to suggest that many male managers are not yet as aware as their female colleagues that traditional 'male' management styles may need to be re-examined (BBC 1990). On the other hand, Still (1988) has shown that the style profile of a woman manager in Australia has 80 per cent correspondence with that of the ideal manager while the male manager's profile has only 50 per cent correspondence.

Figure 26

MALE, FEMALE AND IDEAL MANAGEMENT STYLES

Male Management Style	Female Management Style	Ideal Management Style
Self-Confident	Competent	Competent
Competent	Determined	Knowledgeable
Knowledgeable	Self-Confident	Dependable
Determined	Knowledgeable	Innovative
Competitive	Thorough	Self-Confident
Aggressive	Dependable	Logical
Logical	Competitive	Honest
Dependable	Innovative	Fair
Enterprising	Logical	Thorough
Firm	Honest	Friendly

Reproduced courtesy of Leonie Still

More broadly, our interviewees appear to accept that they have to succeed at the 'male' model of management as well as introducing 'female' styles. In other words, their management styles are androgynous, selecting from a wide range of both 'female' and 'male' characteristics.

Within the constraints of our investigation, it is impossible to conclude that such an androgynous management style benefits both individuals who practise it as well as their organisations. The literature on androgyny has not yet reached a definitive description of the concept, or of its implications for managerial effectiveness. Singer (1976) describes androgyny as being 'the embracing of, and easy flowing between, one's masculine and feminine sides, whether man or woman.' Studies show that individuals who are classified as androgynous (scoring high on both masculine and feminine characteristics) are more psychologically flexible and have a wider range of behaviours (Bem, 1974). Such individuals are less likely to be involved in sex role stereotypes and are more likely to see people in terms of their psychological characteristics rather than in current cultural definitions of masculinity and feminity (Bem, 1985).

While it may seem that such characteristics should contribute to managerial effectiveness, research findings are inconclusive. Motowidlo (1982) finds that some subordinates find an androgynous style very acceptable in their female bosses. But other studies have argued that it may be more advantageous for both male and female leaders to possess primarily 'male' characteristics, because feminine qualities are not generally perceived as contributing to the achievement or retention of power (Powell, 1982). Other critics have seen androgyny as a meaningless ideal (see, for example, Eichler, 1980)

The extent to which our interviewees mention both 'male' and 'female' characteristics in their descriptions of their management styles nevertheless remains striking: they see themselves as flexible and firm, consultative and confrontational, caring and ruthless, competitive and democratic. As we shall see below, some of their strategies and styles as leaders as they describe them are clearly gender neutral: working long hours, being committed to the goals of one's organisation, and seeking challenge are likely to be characteristic traits of leaders in general.

Overall, then, our interviewees' styles as managers appear to be either androgynous or gender neutral. In so far as it is possible to draw a trend from our fifty interviews, we are tempted to suggest that their androgynous characteristics are an integral part of their success. In this respect, as in many facets of their life and career patterns in general, they appear to be more like each other than like either their male counterparts or women in general.

Leadership strategies

What are the largely shared clusters of characteristics and strategies which our interviewees feel have been important in their working lives?

In the first place, nearly all of them are highly committed to the work which they do. Many of them identify to a significant extent with the goals of the organisation for whom they work. Part of their motivation for bearing a heavy burden of work seems to be belief in their organisation, linked with a desire to achieve a high quality in their own work and in that of others for whom they are responsible. In a number of cases — particularly in the public and voluntary sectors — our interviewees' commitment includes appearing to think first of the long- and medium-term needs of their organisations than primarily of how situations could be used to their own benefit.

Secondly, they work extraordinarily hard and often for very long hours — sometimes even to the point, as we shall see in Chapter 5, of threatening their marriages or their own health. Their hard work includes not only carrying out tasks immediately at hand, but also paying careful attention to the manner and style in which they present themselves both intellectually and physically. As we shall see further in Chapter 5, most of our interviewees add to their already heavy workload a substantial commitment to a balanced life, in which they work hard for their families and for their communities, as well as taking part in active leisure pursuits.

Next, our interviewees appear to have an impetus towards action and creativity in both the short and the longer term. As one industrialist comments, 'Whenever I see an opportunity, I take it'. We heard of many instances in which our interviewees have identified needs not currently being met in their organisations and have offered and implemented positive solutions to the problems. Many of our interviewees characterise their own management styles as rooting out problems and dealing with them; they work for longer- rather than shorter-term effectiveness.

Moreover, our interviewees revel in challenge. Their methods are often innovative, breaking the moulds of accepted practice. They challenge ideas and practices which they find unjustifiable, and they push both themselves and their staff to meet those challenges. The same trend marks their career patterns. In most cases, as we saw in Chapter 3, they have experimented with a variety of career paths before finding their major directions, and most of them then tend to change employers and even careers on an average of every four to seven years. They are nearly all trail blazers, at least in the sense of being the first or one of the very few women to hold their particular posts, and they seem to revel in carving out new ways of working effectively.

Fifthly, our interviewees appear to use androgynous styles of management and working. Most of them value highly so-called 'female' management styles. They tend to be inclusive and co-operative, and to acknowledge the needs of others, while always keeping the goals of their organisations clearly in focus. But they can also be competitive, confrontational, ruthless and power seeking. They show a pronounced preference for working on equal terms with both men and women, despite what they often perceive as the obstacles placed in the way of doing so. Many of them say that they feel an obligation to help other women in their organisations, through personal support and through developing equal opportunities policies and practices.

Because they are very highly educated and do not take themselves too seriously, our interviewees appear to be willing to learn from their mistakes and to test theory against practice. Most of them are also committed to the idea and practice of management training in order to develop further their own skills. They are also, on the whole, keenly aware of the need for training of their own staff.

Finally, they are realists. They recognise the constraints that operate on their lives as senior women in Scotland and they work within them, while sometimes trying also to diminish the effect of these restrictions on their own lives and on the lives of other women. As we shall see in greater detail in Chapter 5, they do not try to be 'superwomen'. Acknowledging both their strengths and their limitations, they actively seek (and acknowledge) help — from mentors, from colleagues, and sometimes from their families.

And what of their domestic lives? Are their relationships with husbands and other male partners affected by their working at such senior levels? What decisions have they made — and why — about whether to have children? Do they try to hold together a traditional household in which women are primarily responsible for maintenance of the younger and the older generation as well as, sometimes, of a male partner? From their public we shall now turn to their private lives.

Chapter Five

Leaders as Women

Introduction

So far in this book, we have focused primarily on those facets of our interviewees' experience which tend to be publicly acknowledged — their early upbringing and education, their career patterns and their ways of working in professional or managerial positions. By contrast, in this chapter and the following one, we shall consider more personal and, often, intimate and sensitive matters relating to sex as well as gender. In the present chapter we shall look at our interviewees' relationships with their families and how they spend their leisure time. In Chapter 6, we shall discuss their visions of the future, for themselves, for their sons and daughters, and for other women and men.

We shall consider first the marital circumstances of our interviewees, because such circumstances appear to have had a significant effect on both their private and their public lives. We shall then examine their attitudes towards having children and the experience of those who have decided to become mothers. Next, we shall discuss the use our interviewees make of their leisure time, the extent to which they feel themselves to be under stress, their attitudes towards their own personal appearance as women in senior positions, and how far — if at all — they feel that they have managed to bring all of the competing demands on their time into an appropriate balance.

Marriage

By far the largest proportion of our fifty interviewees have been or are currently married:

Figure 27

MARITAL STATUS

	%
Married	58
Divorced, Separated, Widowed	24
Single	18

No. of Interviewees = 50

How far do these patterns relate to national trends? We have seen at many points in this book that our interviewees tend to be more like one another than like the population as a whole. Do such differences extend to marital status? It appears not. The percentages of those of our interviewees who are single (meaning those who have never married), who have been married to one partner only, who have re-married, and who are divorced or separated, are roughly in line with the percentages in the UK as a whole (*Social Trends*, 1989). The figures are also roughly comparable to those found in other studies of female managers such as Marshall (1984) and Scase and Goffee (1989). It is perhaps worth noting however, that, although our figures are roughly representative of women in the country as a whole as well as of other female managers and senior professionals, the picture created by those proportions would probably be very different for senior men; Scase and Goffee, for instance, found that 95 per cent of their senior male managers were married, as compared with only 55 per cent of the female managers whom they studied.

But what of the actual experience that lies behind the bald figures? When did our interviewees marry? What support have their husbands given? What conflicts have they experienced? And why did a number of them decide never to marry at all?

Decisions to marry

Most studies of women in senior positions have found that they tend to marry later in life than do their more junior counterparts (cf Miles, 1985; Marshall, 1984, Scase and Goffee, 1989). However, of the 72 per cent of our interviewees who are, or have been, married, 61 per cent of those for whom we have such data were married before reaching the age of twenty-five; the average of first marriage for women is now twenty-four in the UK. Because our interview process was not designed to probe the reasons for such patterns, we are unable to offer any evidence for explanations of the trend. It may be that such an unexpected finding is connected with the high degree of experimentation which we have earlier suggested characterises our interviewees in their late teens and, particularly, their twenties.

The experiences of those who married young have, predictably, varied considerably from those who married later. Of the twenty women who married young, nine have been divorced from their first husbands, although a number have since re-married. By contrast, of the thirteen who were aged twenty-five and over on marriage, only two have divorced. Scase and Goffee (1989) have speculated that, where wives embark on careers only after marriage, this often stresses the marriage and can lead to break up and divorce in extreme situations. As we shall see below, such conflict does appear to be most prevalent amongst those of our interviewees who married young. Perhaps, as one of our interviewees suggests:

> It's very important to develop your own identity before marriage . . . I'm amazed at what some of my female friends put up with in marriage.

There appears to be no general strategy in our interviewees' decision to marry. Some interviewees simply assumed that they would marry:

> I always thought I would get married, and I did, at the age of twenty five . . . Having a husband means having a commitment to somebody else and also involves having a more rounded life style.

Others assumed that they would not marry, but did so anyway:

> When I was in my teens, I thought that I would not — and did not want to — get married because I hated almost everything about domestic life, especially housework and the possibility of looking after children. Yet I married at the age of twenty because I couldn't bear the thought that my boyfriend might leave to do his post graduate work thousands of miles away from me.

Nine of our interviewees have never married. The reason which they give most often for this decision is that they believe that the need for mobility — particularly job-related travelling — precludes marriage:

> I live in a flat but am there fairly irregularly. I travel a great deal. The last time I had to go on a business trip, as I shut the door, I said, 'My goodness, I couldn't do this if I were married'.

> I've remained single. It would be very difficult to do my job if I had been married, mainly because of the amount of travel throughout Scotland.

> It would be extremely difficult to undertake the job I do if I were married. I travel all over Scotland and can't afford to turn down jobs.

Cartoon by Viv Quinlan

At first glance, this emphasis by those who are single on the extent to which travel deters them from marriage forms an odd contrast with the fact that many of our married interviewees also do substantial amounts of travelling. Our analysis of the job-related travel of both our single and our married interviewees suggests, in fact, that the assertion that the need to travel is in itself an obstacle to marriage is not upheld by evidence. However, it does appear that one very real deterrent may be, as we have already noted in Chapter 3, the mobility requirements of certain jobs; in many dual-career marriages, major difficulties are often created by the conflicting mobility demands of each partner.

Another deterrent to marriage for senior women may well be the difficulty of sustaining a demanding job and maintaining a traditional household in which women primarily care for the welfare of their immediate family and defer to male decisions. As we shall see below, for

our married and previously married interviewees, the most prevalent form
of marital conflict appears to be that caused by discordance between
women's successful achievement at work and their husbands'
expectations that their wives will play traditional roles. It is thus not
surprising that a number of our single interviewees have clearly thought a
great deal about the implications of marriage, and remain ambivalent
about it for themselves:

> I am now [in my thirties] and wonder whether I ever will be married. I have
> a steady boyfriend but not marriage plans. It annoys me that other
> colleagues — both male and female — jump to conclusions that I must be a
> career woman and that if I'm not married by thirty-seven I never will be and
> never want to be. I still feel ambivalent about marriage. I worry about how I
> could cope with combining work and marriage. Most of the [other female
> professionals in my field] concentrate on local work, whereas I have built up
> all my connections in a Scottish network and would therefore have to be a
> great deal more mobile than many of the other female [professionals] whom
> I know.

For a few of our single interviewees, however, marriage appears to have
been rejected:

> I nearly got married when I was in my early twenties. Now I'm very hard to
> please!

> Marriage can diminish a woman. I haven't lost any kind of dimension in my
> life through not having a husband and children.

EXPERIENCE OF MARRIAGE

But most of our interviewees are, or have been, married. Most of these
who remain married speak of their husband's support in glowing terms.
In the first place, husbands are clearly valued for the emotional and
practical support which they give to their wives' careers:

> I've been greatly helped and supported by my husband, who encouraged me
> to do a Ph.D. Throughout my studying and my career, my husband has
> been a great support. Once or twice when I thought of stopping work he has
> encouraged me to carry on.

> My husband always took pride in my achievements — even if he was
> sometimes unhappy about the price in exhaustion that had to be paid for
> combining them with child care and housework. I always felt that I could
> take any kind of work problem to him and get positive, concrete help with
> it.

> Having a partner has been a great help. I greatly enjoy going home in the
> evenings and being able to talk over the problems of the day.

My husband gives me both emotional stability and the practical stability that I need. I get a great deal of help from him.

We have a close marriage, although my husband is very different from me. One of my daughters has said that my husband is like a well and I am like a fountain.

My husband has been a great resource and always supportive.

Secondly, many of our interviewees report that their husbands offer practical assistance on the domestic front as well as help with professional work and emotional support:

My husband is extremely domesticated and is very encouraging to me in my career.

I have a marvellous husband who is very supportive and helps me at home. He also comes to functions with me.

The only criticism I could make of my husband is his lack of ability to make decisions. Apart from that he is extremely supportive of my work and very domesticated.

We shall return to the question of the organisation of child care and housework later in this chapter. Meanwhile, it is worth noting that our findings about the importance generally of marriage in the careers of senior women in Scotland are reinforced by very recent studies of female managers elsewhere. Scase and Goffee (1989), for instance, find that 'many [female managers] feel their career chances are improved with a carefully 'screened' and 'selected' partner rather than if they choose to remain single . . . Most women managers cope with any potential conflicts between their work and home lives by . . . choosing to live with partners who are prepared to accommodate the demands of their two careers.'

Despite the generally positive assessments of their experience of marriage, however, at least one interviewee holds a rather more mixed view:

Being married and having a family has definitely helped me in my career. It's given me a much closer insight into many of the problems that face other women.

It is to these problems that we shall now turn.

CONFLICTS

The problems experienced in the marriages of our interviewees have, of course, appeared primarily in the relationships of those who have been divorced or separated. One major source of tension between partners, however, appears to characterise both broken as well as current marriages: the problems created by the need for geographical mobility in dual-career marriages. We have already dealt with the impact of this issue on the career patterns of our interviewees in Chapter 3, but we propose to return to it here because it appears to be such a potent source of serious problems.

There are relatively fewer senior positions available within commuting distance of one another in Scotland than in, say, the south east of England. Dual-career marriages in Scotland can therefore be placed under acute pressure when the geographical mobility requirements of each partner are incompatible. An important career opportunity may open for a husband in Aberdeen, when a wife has just begun work in a new senior position in Edinburgh. To some extent the fact that such a large proportion of the population of Scotland live within the central belt stretching from Glasgow to Edinburgh means that it is often feasible for couples to work, for instance, simultaneously in Stirling and Dundee (although the needs of children may well militate against such commuting). But sometimes places of work simply cannot be connected by any conventional (or affordable) means. How have our interviewees dealt with basic conflicts arising from demands for mobility?

Severally live physically apart from their husbands for most of the time; they have long distance marriages:

> My marriage has always been a very equal partnership. My husband works in England and we meet at weekends. This works fairly well. Having some space and time to myself is becoming increasingly important to me.

> We have a main house in Edinburgh, but I also have a flat in [another city]. My husband's job is in [England] so we meet at weekends. We have help in the house and a gardener, because with that lifestyle we need it.

In other cases, our married interviewees have accepted that their careers will have to fit around their husband's geographical circumstances:

> If I were offered [a post] in Aberdeen or Inverness, this would be impossible for me. I do hope that when an offer comes it will be in the central belt of Scotland.

> Mobility has never been an issue for us. I've never been tempted by anything outside the [area where I live], and my husband will work here too all his life. There was only one time that he might have done otherwise. He decided not to — but on grounds other than my job.

Marriages are also put under strain by other facets of career decisions. To a very significant extent, those of our interviewees whose marriages have broken up give their careers as a major — if not the most important — factor in separating from their husbands. Sometimes the fact that both partners worked long hours is seen as a contributing factor:

> I was married for five years. My husband was also in [the same professional field], and we both worked very long hours. Part of the reason for our break-up was career-linked: because of the hours we worked, we saw less and less of each other and drifted apart. But there were no bad feelings, and we are still quite good friends.

More typically, however, considerable strain was created in our interviewees' marriages by their undertaking either work or study or both:

> I applied to [university] to read law and was offered a place [in my thirties]. I thoroughly enjoyed the course, but it put a great deal of pressure on our marriage.

Some marriages suffered, our interviewees believe, through wives' commitment to their careers:

> I am separated from my husband. Part of the reason for the separation was my deep involvement in, and commitment to, my career.

In particular, divergences between the extent of husbands' and wives' career successes are seen as a major factor in breaking up marriages:

> When we returned to Scotland after eight years of marriage, my husband had to re-train [in his profession] and had difficulty finding work . . . Our marriage broke up, caused by our slowly drifting apart as a couple, exacerbated by my husband's lack of work contrasting with my own successful career development.

> My husband [in a manual occupation] felt jealous of my climb to fame. He started drinking heavily and blamed it on my working. I gave up work for six months but things didn't settle, and I realised that the drinking related to his problems rather than to myself. So I decided to return to work . . . My marriage has recently ended. It has opened up new doors to me. I'm undertaking a part-time degree at [a university] — a project I could never have undertaken if I were married.

Wives' dislike of domestic life as contrasted with husbands' preferences for traditional households is also cited by a number of interviewees as a significant factor in the break-up of their marriages:

I was married at university and tried to play the traditional role of housewife, whilst also trying to develop my career early on, studying for a post-graduate course . . . It didn't work out. I didn't like it. I certainly didn't like doing the ironing. Although at the end my husband walked out on me, in many ways it was a relief.

When my first husband left me, I was a full-time post-graduate student, very ambitious to continue working at university; he was also a student. At the time it seemed to me very significant that he left me to be with a woman who had given up a promising academic career to become a full-time mother. When I married again a few years later, it seemed as if nearly all our rows (not that there were many of them) revolved around what my husband saw as the conflict between my role as a wife, and later as a mother, and my commitment to working as an academic. There were rows over meals that were late because I had been held up at departmental meetings; there were quarrels because I did not do enough for his international guests because of the pressure of my own work; there were sometimes quite desperate arguments over how tired I was getting through trying to manage both a full-time job and young children.

In other cases, threats to a marriage, or its actual ending, served as an important motivating factor in undertaking a career:

I was not career orientated when I was younger and never viewed [my profession] as a career when I joined it. I don't think I would be in my present job if I were still married. I certainly wouldn't have bothered to [complete a qualification] — it didn't seem important when I was married.

At this stage it was very important to my self image to get back out to work. And I felt strongly that I had to get some financial independence. My marriage was going through a crisis.

Those whose marriages remain intact, however, tend to acknowledge the strains of dual-career partnerships, but to believe that marriage will always have strains of some sort anyway:

The practical side of working and having kids does put certain stresses on our marriage, but such a relationship is anyway potentially full of stresses and strains.

Working has put pressure on my marriage, but I feel strongly that there would have been different pressures on my husband and me if I hadn't worked.

Despite the strains on our marriage because of my combining a career and children, the marriage has been strengthened by the fact that I am financially independent of my husband. I stay with him out of choice, not necessity.

Despite the complexity of such marriages, many of our interviewees have had children. Perhaps to an even greater extent than in deciding whether to marry, the question of whether and when to have children seems to have been critical in their lives, partly, of course, because of the enormous time commitment required by parenting. We shall now turn to factors in that decision, and shall take a look at the experience of those who decided to become mothers.

Dependents

CHILDREN
Of our fifty interviewees, nearly half (48 per cent) have children, although several are still sufficiently young to start families. Of those who have children, the majority have two children:

Figure 28

NUMBER OF CHILDREN

	%
One	17
Two	52
Three	17
Four	13

No. of Interviewees = 24

Apart from one single women who has adopted two daughters, all of those who have had children have done so while they were married, although a number are now single parents. The proportions of women with one, two, three or four children are roughly equal to the UK population as a whole. Where our interviewees diverge sharply from the national picture, however, is in their very high proportion of childlessness: it has been estimated that only 20 per cent of women born in 1955 onwards will not have children (*Social Trends*, 1989), but 52 per cent of our interviewees have no children.

Although they are unlike the population as a whole in this respect, the relatively high proportions of our interviewees who are childless resemble some other findings about senior women, although overall our interviewees seem to be more likely to have children than many other studies have found. Comparable levels of childlessness to those of our interviewees are found in Miles (1985), who found that 50 per cent of her sample of senior women were childless, and Sutherland (1985), who found that 57 per cent of her sample of female academics — at all levels of the university hierarchy — were childless. More typically, SIACE (1990) found that 73 per cent of its female managers and aspirant managers (who were, however, slightly younger than our interviewees) were childless, while Marshall (1984) found an even higher figure of 87 per cent childlessness amongst the women managers whom she interviewed. Scase and Goffee (1989) found that 80 per cent of their junior and middle female managers were childless.

DECISIONS ABOUT WHETHER TO HAVE CHILDREN

As one might expect, our interviewees' decisions about whether to have children appear to be based on a wide range of motivations and factors. Of those who have decided to remain childless, the main reason appears to be their belief that working full-time at a serious career would potentially conflict with motherhood:

> I have no children, by choice. I could have worked and had children, but it would have presented me with many problems.

> I did a great deal of travelling in my job. If I had been married or had children, it would have caused many problems.

Most of those who have remained childless speak of being happy with their choice or, at least, of recognising that they do not wish to become mothers:

> I have no children and am unlikely to change things in any significant way . . . I'm happy with the balance in my life.

> My husband and I do not wish to have children.

> We have no children, partly by choice, partly by chance. I doubt whether I'll have children now.

All of these women who have decided not to have children clearly have much in common with Scase and Goffee's women managers who 'cope with any potential conflicts between their work and home lives by not having children'.

A few interviewees, however, are actively considering whether and when to have children:

> The big question now is whether to have children.

> I've been starting to think seriously about my next career move, because I

know that it has biological implications. I'm now in my mid thirties, and if I don't make a deliberate decision to have children within the next few years I shan't have any at all.

The next big decision is whether to have children. I think I would like to have them, but I'm not sure if I would want to have them by my present husband.

We have been married for nine years, but have no children *yet*.

Of those who have decided to have children, a number were initially attracted to the life of a wife and mother within the framework of a traditional marriage:

Soon after we married I became pregnant and had our only child — a son. I thought I would settle in the house well and looked forward to bringing up my son.

I was married at seventeen and left work when I had my first baby at eighteen. I now have three boys and a girl.

Others knew from the beginning that full time motherhood was not for them, but nevertheless wanted children:

I knew that I didn't want children as a full-time vocation. My children are more important to me than my career, but they are not the only thing.

I had wanted to have children for about five years before my son was born; indeed, sometimes I used to fantasise about having a large household full of children, and I always liked having lots of children around for parties. Once I had our second child, however, the reality of trying to manage children and a full time job took over, and I decided to have a sterilisation rather than risk the possibility of a third child.

To some extent, these contrasting decisions about whether and when to have children reflect differences in the predominantly working-class or middle-class childhoods of our interviewees. Most of our married interviewees from working class backgrounds opted for early marriage and full-time child rearing, often in their teens. Their middle class counterparts tended to marry later and to be much more likely to take partial or no career breaks on the birth of their children. To a significant extent, of course, these patterns are connected with the relative lack of affordable good quality child care in Scotland. For a mother of young children without higher education and on a low wage, the only choices usually available are part time work or full time motherhood.

Another important factor may be the changing trends in women's beliefs about whether women with children should work at all. As *Social Trends* (1989) shows, in 1987, as in 1965, no woman believed that a married woman with children under school age ought to work (as differentiated from being free to work). The proportion of those who believe that 'it's up to her', however, rose from 5 per cent in 1965 to 26 per cent in 1987, with a further 29 per cent in 1987 believing that a mother of young children should work only if she needs the money. The percentage of those who believe that a married woman with children under school age should stay at home has dropped from 78 per cent in 1965 to 45 per cent in 1987, while those who believe that a married woman with children at school should stay at home have dropped from 20 per cent in 1965 to 7 per cent in 1987. These figures from *Social Trends* (1989) need to be seen in the light of the finding in Strathclyde Region in Scotland that only 24 per cent of those mothers currently at home would choose to be at home if adequate childcare were available (Scott, 1989b).

But what has been the effect on the lives of our interviewees of deciding to have children? And what has been the effect on their children of mothers deciding to work full-time at demanding, even greedy, careers? We shall now turn to these questions.

EFFECTS OF CHILDREN

Nearly all of our interviewees with children speak in overwhelmingly positive terms about their experience of bringing up children, although they are also acutely aware of the resultant pressures on time:

> Throughout my career so far I've had lots of small successes. My greatest pride, however, is in my children.

> My [adopted] children have coloured and enriched my life.

> My children are one of the two focal points of my life — the other is my work. They have been the source of some of the greatest joy *and* the greatest anxiety in my life. I know that they have both felt as they were growing up that I should have spent more time with them, and I have often felt torn between their claims on my time and the competing claims of a demanding job. But I also know that I would far rather live with that sense of competing claims than either not have children or not have a career.

> Having a child has given me stability and support in what is often a rather frantic job.

So overwhelmingly important are what our interviewees see as the needs of their children that in a few — but not many — cases, they have made career decisions based on what they have seen as the primary needs of their children:

After my daughter was born, I left work. I felt that, with two children, I should. Things were better then financially too . . . Later I thought about training in home economics simply because it could lead to a job that would fit in with school holidays.

I went to [a college of education] for a year because teaching would be a good career for a mother, but I hated it . . . As my husband worked shifts and I had two young daughters, I had to look at courses and careers which would fit in with my domestic responsibilities.

In several other cases, taking part in voluntary community activities connected with their experience of raising young children proved to be an important factor in interviewees' later careers in paid employment:

I've always been an organiser. When my children were young, I started the first play group in the area.

My husband and I moved to the Netherlands where he was working. I had our only child there — a daughter. But I found it very stifling — I didn't speak Dutch; we lived in a small rural community; and I was lonely. My husband was then offered a job in the Middle East, and we moved there. This time I was determined not to be isolated. I joined the National Housewives Register and ran a section of it where we lived.

Due to the relative lack in Scotland of affordable high quality child care, most of our interviewees who worked full-time in the sixties and seventies when their children were young employed private full time child minders or nannies:

I used child minders when the children were little.

Until my youngest child was at school, we had a full-time nanny. I don't think that they've suffered as a result in any way . . . They're perhaps slightly more independent than other children might be at their age, but I don't think that's any bad thing.

Until my youngest child was in nursery school (which she started at the age of two), we had full-time help at home; afterwards, I had a series of part-time helpers. How the children felt about them was always very important to me; I am especially pleased that they now go out of the way to visit our housekeeper, who has been with us for ten years, and who treats the children as if they were her own.

In those families with younger children there appears to be a slight shift towards more equal sharing of child care between both parents:

> We had two children one soon after the other. My husband gave up his job to care for the children.

The predominant pattern, however, appears still to be employing full-time private help with young children, with both parents taking a share in domestic work when they are at home. Perceptions of who actually does most at home vary:

> My husband is a positive help, although he probably thinks he does more than he does on the domestic front.

> My husband was always wonderfully responsive to the children and excelled at playing with them, at introducing them to new experiences: he was a much better parent than I was in those respects. But I always seemed to end up doing the routine and very time-consuming sort of child care — changing nappies, dressing the children, preparing their food, tidying up their toys. When they were older, I usually drove them to activities, helped with their music practice, shopped with them for clothes, and so on.

In the case of the few of our interviewees who are now single parents, however, even such partial sharing of child care is usually not available. As we have already seen in Chapter 3, for this small group of mothers, demands invariably exceed the time available:

> Bringing up two children as a single parent while working full-time at a challenging job has often seemed like a nightmare, especially when the demands of work clashed with the needs of the children. I've managed only really by working almost every hour of every day and by having almost no leisure time for myself. But in retrospect I wouldn't ever have been prepared to let any of it go.

It is thus not surprising that none of our single parents have become so by choice — say, by deliberately choosing to have a child without a live-in partner. The decision to separate from husbands where children were involved is clearly one taken extremely seriously by our interviewees, as an excerpt from one of them suggests:

> At that stage the children were eleven and eight, and I took a full-time job. By then our marriage was under pressure. My husband was mentally ill, and relations with him and between him and the children were very strained. I decided to leave. It was a decision I did not take lightly and which was very traumatic for me.

As well as the effect of children on their mothers' lives, the other major issue is, of course, the effect of working mothers on their children's lives.

Because we did not attempt to speak to the children of our interviewees, we are unable directly to assess the effects on our interviewees' children. As the excerpts above have suggested, the mothers themselves tend to feel that, at worst, their children have not suffered from their mothers' working and, indeed, might even have benefited from it. Although a number of interviewees with children referred to the pressure on their time created by combining full-time work with raising children, only one interviewee with children used the word 'guilt' in connection with her working full-time while raising children.

But such views from our interviewee mothers are necessarily self-interested. The sole impartial indicator available from our interviewees is evidence about children's participation in higher education. Nearly all of those of our interviewees' children who are old enough to be in, or to have completed, higher education have done so, despite the fact that, as we noted in Chapter 2, not all of our interviewees themselves had proceeded directly to a higher education. A number of our interviewees also made comments such as 'My children have all done well' and 'I am very ambitious for my children.'

On the whole, then, the actual experience of children by their mothers (aside, perhaps, from those women who are single parents) does not appear to support the fears of those interviewees who have decided not to have children because of the problems that they believe would result. Nevertheless, the formidable barriers often placed against working mothers by the lack of affordable, high quality child care provision in Scotland are well recognised by our interviewees. As two interviewees summed it up:

> The major problem that women, men and society have to come to terms with is women's child-bearing role.

> The most crucial issue for the 1990s is that of child care.

CARE OF OTHER DEPENDANTS

The care of parents and other elderly relatives is also becoming increasingly important as a factor in the working lives of our interviewees. However, our data about the care of other dependants — usually parents — is much less full than for many other areas covered by the interviews. What follows below is therefore only a sketch of some of the impressions which we have gained through analysis of the interviews.

For many of our interviewees, family responsibilities include the care of ageing relatives of their own and their husbands:

> I believe in the extended family. My father-in-law lived with us for eight years before his death; my husband's aunt is now about to come.

I had just applied for, and got, a job as senior lecturer when my father- and mother-in-law came to stay. The children were only nine and eleven. So I was doing a full time job but had to leave lunch for everyone and then cook a meal for six every night.

And, analogously to the sense of responsibility for dependent children which led some of our interviewees to take full or partial career breaks while their children were young, so also some of our interviewees have felt direct conflict between the demands of their professional work and the need to care for elderly relatives:

I gave up my job [at a senior level] mainly because of my mother's ill health.

My mother is now eighty-seven and in a nursing home. Each time I visit she begs me to stop work and look after her . . . I'm concerned about the fact that she wants me to stop work, and expects it of me.

Both my parents are still alive, and I have a certain amount of responsibility for them . . . There are major problems for women with regard to caring for children and caring for older people. Time off for carers is really necessary. These are really neglected areas. There should be a lot more part-time work available and more help available and more recognitiion of the problem.

In a social — and currently a political — climate often unsupportive of the needs of children and elderly people, those of our interviewees who have taken on responsibility for both children and elderly relatives have somehow managed to sustain what must often appear like impossible levels of commitment. In particular, it is notable that it is just those interviewees who already carry heavy burdens of time commitment — such as those in particularly demanding jobs who have young or adolescent children — who have taken on the additional responsibility of caring for elderly relatives. In this respect our interviewees tend to fall into two major types — those who appear to be primarily committed to a career, who tend to be single or married without children, on the one hand, and, on the other, those who are highly committed to their career but who have also undertaken responsibility for children and, often, elderly relatives as well.

Particularly for those women who sustain what appear to be almost intolerable burdens of responsibility, is there anything left in their lives after they have met their immediate obligations to their employers and their families? Do they even have any leisure time? How much stress are they under and how do they cope with it? How does the pattern differ for those with fewer explicit commitments? And, in the midst of so many competing claims for their attention, how do they feel about themselves as women? We shall now attempt to complete our picture of their personal lives by examining these questions.

Leisure

In practice, distinctions between the use of leisure for personal purposes and the use of it for housework and child care, and distinctions between child care and housework, are difficult to sustain. Parents may spend their holidays on the beach not because that is their own preference but for the children; tidying away toys, washing children's clothes and preparing their meals are amongst many activities which are difficult to decide whether to place with child care or with housework.

Regardless of distinctions or overlaps, however, it appears as if our interviewees share the general experience of women in the UK that women carry more responsibility than men for domestic work. In the UK as a whole, where both partners work, in 72 per cent of households women mainly carry out domestic tasks (*Social Trends*, 1989). A much higher percentage of women believe that tasks should be shared equally than actually have them shared (ibid). This picture is by and large that reported by our interviewees:

> [My husband] is a great moral support, but when it comes to practicalities he's not so good. But to be fair with him, he's not the type of man who sits about the house and does nothing. He doesn't do very much because he isn't here very much — he works long hours . . . I do a lot more housework than he does . . . but I get no pleasure out of doing it.

> My husband hasn't stood in my way, but he hasn't given me any great amount of support and encouragement. He expected that the housework would be carried on as before, by me, even once I went to college.

> My husband would always say that he did his fair share of housework, and he was very good at things like cooking, laying the table, loading the dishwasher. But his idea of how to help with mountains of washing and ironing was simply to say that it could easily wait until the next day!

Interviewees' feelings about housework vary considerably, as the excerpts below show. Most interviewees appear to accept it as an unpleasant necessity, and many have devised strategies for lessening as far as possible the amount of it that they have to do:

> I've always hated housework and do as little as possible, consistent with having a reasonably tidy and safe house. I don't believe that one adult should routinely service the needs of others who are capable of looking after themselves. So, from a very early stage, I have tried to teach the children to do their own housework, such as washing clothes, ironing, changing beds and so on.

We have help in the house and a gardener.

A cleaning woman and my husband help with our domestic chores.

In rare cases housework is seen as a form of release from stress:

> I have no domestic help — by choice. I find physical work like housework a
> kind of therapy.

And what of the other uses of that part of our interviewees' time which
is not spent on professional or managerial employment? The first
characteristic is that, as one might expect, there is not much of it. The
evidence generally is overwhelming that women in full time employment
have the least leisure time of all groups (Deem, 1986; *Social Trends*,
1989). We did not, however, attempt to quantify the amount of time
spent by our interviewees on their personal leisure. Rather, we asked,
'What do you do to relax in your spare time?' We have analysed below
the replies to this question which we received from the forty-two
interviewees who answered it.

Despite the very heavy pressure on their time, most of our interviewees
appear to lead very active lives in the time that is not committed to their
jobs or their domestic responsibilities, as may be seen from the table
below:

Figure 29

TYPES OF LEISURE ACTIVITIES

	%
Sports	64
Arts	43
Organisations	40
Academic	26
Travel/Holidays	19
Friends/Entertaining	17
Gardening	10
Others	17

No. of Interviewees = 42

To begin with, it is worth noting that these explicitly identified activities
probably do not reflect the full extent of the leisure activities of our
interviewees. It seems unlikely, for instance, that only 17 per cent of them
have any friends and that none of them ever watches television or listens
to the radio! The list should therefore be seen as indicative rather than
comprehensive. It does, nevertheless, serve to add weight to our earlier

findings both about the generally high level of activity of our interviewees and about the extent to which, in many respects, they tend to resemble one another.

Most typically, interviewees report a range of activities in their spare time, and every interviewee reports at least one form of leisure activity, with some reporting activities under almost every heading. Nearly two-thirds report active involvement in at least one sport. Most often interviewees speak about hill walking or walking, but they also mention a very wide range of other sports, including aerobics, swimming, golf, riding, skiing, wind surfing, and sailing. Substantial numbers mention taking part in the arts, either as performers (particularly of music) or as audience. The organisations referred to in the table on the previous page cover a wide range of involvement and types of activity. One interviewee, for instance, has helped to found an AIDS charity, while another goes on religious retreats. The heading of 'academic' includes the fact that a number of interviewees are mature students, reflecting the tendency which we noted earlier to continue to study well beyond the initial qualification at higher education level; it also includes taking part in adult education courses and serious reading.

In the light of our earlier findings about children, it is not surprising that women without children or with grown-up children tend to report the most number of activities. By contrast, a characteristic comment from a mother of two small children is:

> I don't have very much spare time, and this is a constant problem for me. So I've lost out on tennis, entertaining etc since the birth of our second child.

Another interviewee explicitly recognises loss of leisure as a major price to be paid for an active professional life while her children were young:

> I have so many different things that I like doing — and that I would like to try if I could — that I really don't know how to begin to answer the question. It's only recently, as the children have become adults, that I've really been able to explore what I like to do for myself. Previously, all our leisure activities were geared primarily around what the children would also enjoy. So we went swimming, played tennis, went to children's theatre and concerts, to museums and so on. Now one of the pleasures of having grown-up children is that I can finally share with them those things that I really like doing — such as going to the opera or art galleries — though I haven't yet persuaded them of the pleasures of hill walking!

Another feels that:

> I have a very full life, with my work and my domestic problems, so there's not much time for leisure. I always look forward to holidays!

In general, then, it appears as if our interviewees are as active in their personal leisure as they have time to be, with those who do not have major domestic commitments undertaking an especially wide range of activities. One childless interviewee, for instance, reports her involvement in politics, voluntary organisations, tap dancing, socialising and music. As a result of such high levels of activity at work, at home and at leisure, are our interviewees therefore under stress? And, if so, how do they cope with it?

STRESS AND BALANCE

Most of our interviewees report feeling stress in at least one part of their lives. It is notable, however, that the stress appears to derive primarily from work or from family problems rather than from any sense of conflict between those two major commitments; the exception, as in so many cases, is that of single parents, who report feeling stressed because of the extent of the competing demands on their time.

A number of our interviewees report feeling stressed because of problems at home, primarily those related to husbands or parents:

> Both my parents are still alive, and I have a certain amount of responsibility for them. Coping with them is stressful.

> At certain times I've been under a great deal of stress — especially when my marriage was breaking up.

Some actively prefer working under stressful conditions:

> I prefer to work under stress. I work better under pressure. If things are too quiet, I find that I sit behind a desk and end up shuffling papers.

> I occasionally feel under stress, but usually revel in it.

> Deadlines make me stressed, but it's the only way I can work.

Nearly all of our interviewees have tactics for dealing with their stress:

> I feel under stress a great deal of the time. I find that the best way to cope is massage and talking to people I'm close to.

> Time on my own is important. If I'm stressed, I enjoy swimming or relaxing in a bath.

> At times I do suffer from stress. The best way to relieve it is to achieve something. Laughter is also a great help.

I enjoy active sports. I find that tap dancing is a good way to relieve stress.

At times, going out to work is itself seen as a form of escape from a major source of domestic stress:

> My job kept me sane, because I wouldn't have wanted to be in the house all day — my father- and mother-in-law argued constantly!

> A major reason why I returned to work was the stress in my life because of my unhappy marriage.

But, in contrast to those interviewees whose domestic lives provide one potent source of stress, for most others, families are a source of relief from stress:

> I do get tired. My job is not especially stressful. Usually I find that coming home and doing something physical with my children helps greatly . . . I know that I'm totally tired whey they just annoy me . . . Usually I find them a great release and a great help to me.

> I cope with stress by talking to my husband — he is a good listener.

> I know that my [illness] is stress-related. I talk to my husband about problems and drink cups of tea.

As we have noted earlier, the stress experienced by single parents remains a major factor in their lives as long as the children are young:

> At times I have found the stress of working full-time at a demanding job and bringing up two young children on my own almost intolerable. I've sometimes felt as if I were a juggler trying to keep an unreasonable number of balls in the air. I used to be afraid that, if I relaxed my vigilance and attention even for a moment, the whole lot would come tumbling to the ground.

Despite their sometimes feeling stressed, however, most of our interviewees are reasonably or entirely happy with the balance in their lives:

Figure 30

ATTITUDES TOWARDS BALANCE IN ONE'S LIFE

	%
Happy with Balance	46
Happy Generally with Reservations	26
Unhappy with Balance	18
Not Known	10

No. of Interviewees = 50

Those who are happy with the balance in their lives have often made deliberate decisions to prevent work from spilling over into the rest of their lives:

> I want to do a good job and have a good career, but I don't want it to be my whole life. If this means staying at a lower level, so be it.

> My [company] is part — but only part — of my life.

> I try to have a balance in my life, and my husband and I have certain 'rules' about working at home. The early evening is a precious part of the day when we always try to be together.

> I have been a very fortunate person to have had the opportunities that I've had. I've decided to take early retirement. I have done a great deal, and my enthusiasm is waning. There are a number of different types of experiences which I would like to develop. By retiring I will have time to do so.

Those who are in any way unhappy with the balance almost always see the imbalance as created by the very large demands of their work on their time, and, occasionally, by inappropriate spilling over of public into private life:

> I'm happy with the balance in my life, apart from phone calls in the middle of the night from my employer, who promised that he would never contact me at weekends!

> [The balance in my life] is not quite what I would like. I don't have enough time for my children or for myself . . . I'd really like to work for about four days a week, but you don't get jobs of four days a week.

> I can be involved in ten hour days seven days a week, depending on contracts.

> I am a workaholic and have to make a conscious effort not to let my work impinge on my private life. Once when I found myself correcting a report whilst at the opera, I realised that things had got slightly out of hand!

> I spend more time at work than most people and more than I would really like to. It's a very demanding job — I can be on call in the evenings and at weekends.

> I find it very difficult to separate work from my personal life.

Above all, a number of our interviewees warn against being seduced by the myth of the 'superwoman' who can have, and do, it all in apparent ease:

The myth of superwoman is a dangerous image for women to project.

My main advice for all young girls would be not to be taken in by the myth of superwomen.

The idea of superwomen creates an impossible goal for anyone who does not have the kind of money needed to buy time in a major way. Those of us who live on only what we earn ourselves usually can't afford to employ enough other people who can do all of our domestic work, most of our children care, all of our social organising and so on, for us. I also don't think that most people want to lead that kind of vicarious life at home.

If they wish not to project an image of superwomen, then, what kind of image of themselves as women do our interviewees present? How much does their image matter to them? Do they care very much about their physical appearance? And how much do they think that such things are important for them as women in senior positions? We shall now look briefly at these highly sensitive areas where private and public personae meet.

IMAGES OF SUCCESS

As we have already noted in Chapter 3, our interviewees appear to be highly conscious of the importance of physical presentation and to work hard on their appearance. They also forthrightly express approval of women who make the best of themselves and many frankly admit that they spend a great deal of money on clothes. Most of them conform to conventional images of attractiveness in women: most are slim; they tend to look younger than they are; their hair is well cut; they wear discreet make up; and they dress in well-cut, attractive clothes.

Indeed, an indication of how important their appearance is to them appears in the fact that so many of them comment on this factor, although we did not specifically ask a question about it. Many feel that it is hard to over state the importance of how a woman looks:

Image is extremely important for a woman.

I like women who are good-looking and well dressed.

Image is very important; you should dress for the job you want to have, not the job you have.

I like women who are well presented but not glossily packaged.

Nearly all of our interviewees put into practice such beliefs about the overwhelming importance of personal appearance:

Image is important. I like to be well dressed.

Image is very important. I spent large sums of money on my wardrobe.

A number have visited colour consultants. One woman reports that:

> I've visited a colour consultant and have now changed my whole dress and colour sense. Now I look in the mirror and I like what I see. It's given me immeasurable confidence in myself, which I otherwise lacked. I feel no guilt in spending two or three hundred pounds on a dress for work.

Interviewees are also conscious of the advantages of those facets of their appearance about which they can do nothing, such as their height. All but four of our interviewees are average or above average in height, and most are conscious of their size as a positive advantage:

> If people remember you, you get yourself known. Being tall helps you being remembered.

> Being tall is a great help in my job. Small women in [my profession] often struggle for recognition and acceptance.

> It helps to be big.

> Height and image are important for women.

> Being tall helps, as I am remembered well, both within the company and outwith it.

Frank pleasure also emerges as a factor in looking good:

> I'm good to myself. I treat myself to a weekend at Stobo Castle, to getting my hair done, to expensive clothes.

> I was very impressionable during the development of feminism in the seventies, so I've always felt slightly ashamed of the fact that I spend time thinking about how I look and what I wear. My husband used to tease me that the colours I wore always gave an impression of being planned (they were) and that my clothes were always carefully ironed. The truth is that I get pleasure out of looking good. And I've come to believe that dressing well is one way of saying to people that they matter, that you care enough about them to want to please them.

Two of our interviewees, however, were noticeably less well dressed than the others. This decision not to care about dressing well appears to be deliberate:

I reject power dressing. I hate getting dressed up and literally grab the first piece of clothing I can find each morning.

With these two exceptions, however, our interviewees appear to take pleasure in their appearance as women, as well as recognising the importance of their appearance for its effect on their careers. Some of them also appear to believe that achievement and power in themselves are one source of their own sexual attractiveness:

> When I was at university women who did well academically were seen as being somehow sexually undesirable. Now I think that women with power are quite often more sexually desirable.

As far as we can tell, the feeling expressed by one of them could stand for nearly all:

> I am proud of being a woman.

Conclusion

As we shall see further in the following chapter, this clear delight in being female is not always straightforward in its implications. Some of our interviewees, for instance, feel a strong bond with other women; others appear to view their own femininity primarily as one useful attribute on the road to achievement and power. Given such different views, what visions of the future do our interviewees have? What kind of advice would they offer to girls about strategies to maximise their own potential in what most perceive as the largely alien, or even hostile, world of male dominance in senior positions? We shall consider these wider issues in the following chapter before proceeding, in the conclusion, to consider what general factors appear to have been important in the professionally successful lives of our interviewees and how more women might also be encouraged to flourish.

Chapter Six

Nurturing the Future

Introduction

As analysis throughout this book has suggested, our interviewees tend to have a highly developed consciousness about being successful women in the largely male dominated world of public life in Scotland. Most of them acknowledge the pervasive effect of gender on their career patterns, their professional and managerial lives, and their private experience. Most of them celebrate being female in almost all facets of their lives. The majority who have partners speak warmly and lovingly of them. Those who have children speak of delight and pride in them. Interviewees tend to believe that their management styles include female as well as male characteristics, and they take pleasure in their physical appearance.

How far is such a delight in being female primarily an individual feeling and how far does it extend to empathising with, and supporting, other women? Do our interviewees feel any sense of responsibility for nurturing other women? Do they think that the main characteristics of their experience as successful professional women are unique or can they offer advice to girls who are now starting to confront some of the same kinds of choices that they themselves experienced many years ago? What do they think that the future holds for women in Scotland? We shall now explore what our interviewees told us about these implications of their experience.

Advice to girls

One of our interview questions asked what advice, if any, interviewees would like to offer to young girls as a result of their own experience as professional women. The results of asking this question were, to be frank, somewhat disappointing. Even those interviewees who had prepared in substantial depth for the interview questions tended to stumble over their replies to this question, and answers as a whole tend not to be illuminating. Interviewees appear mainly and predictably to suggest that girls should follow in their footsteps by acquiring professional qualifications, aiming for the top regardless of barriers in the way, and being determined to succeed.

In one important respect, however, our interviewees do offer advice to be different from how they had themselves been as girls. They stress heavily the need to conceive as a working professional life as a career, in significant contrast to the way in which many interviewees during their own years as students and immediately afterwards had not done so.

> I would certainly encourage girls to get professional qualifications of some sort — as good as they could get. I think that's crucial. I would also point out to them that the chances are that they will work for most of their lives by choice or necessity . . . Therefore they will want to get into something that will give them good career prospects.

> My advice to girls would be to plan for a career in something that will last.

> I have never really had a career plan; many of my moves have just happened. Luck has played a big part in my career . . . My advice to girls would be to have a career plan.

> All the evidence shows that, other things being equal, women need higher qualifications than men to reach the same positions. So I'd advise all girls to go for as high qualifications as they can, preferably before starting paid employment, because it's much more difficult to do it as a mature student. I'd also advise them to aim at high but achievable goals and to take a great deal of care over how they present themselves and their ideas. Finally, I would like to encourage all girls to assume that they have a full choice of career possibilities and patterns, rather than presupposing that certain careers are more appropriate for either men or women.

> I would advise girls to get as good qualifications as possible and not to be diverted, to choose something that will be currency for the future and that they would enjoy doing.

Drawing on their own experience, interviewees offer detailed advice about what they believe are effective career strategies:

> Do something that makes you happy. Make your own decisions, try not to have regrets. Project yourself to the age of seventy and think, will I be happy with what I've done? Try to identify people who can and will help you. Cultivate useful people and make yourself visible. Make your wishes known. And don't be disappointed if you don't get what you wanted first time. Luck plays a part in any career, but effort is also very important.

Apply for jobs before you're ready. Applications for job interviews are a way of flagging yourself up even if at first you're not successful. You have to be prepared to push yourself forward.

Women must start to do more for themselves. If you're going to compete, you must compete at the same level as men . . . You have to know your job, do it as well as you can and be confident in your own ability.

In order to get on in a career, you must find out the patterns of the organisation. Once you know the patterns you can start changing things. It's probably easier for women to get on in a large organisation with a formal open management structure such as local government than in smaller, more informally run businesses. I also think that a woman is more likely to get promoted internally rather than being promoted externally. Being an external candidate for a job you are an unknown quantity; being a women doesn't help the situation.

If you're ambitious, you have to be prepared to take part in informal networking and socialising off the job.

It is important to speak out early on when invited to join a committee. Make your position clear and let members see that you are not just a token woman. Think about the issue — not yourself.

If you want to get on you must break from the pack. Although for many women it's pleasant to spend time talking, for instance, to secretaries or clerical workers, if you're keen and ambitious you must be prepared to be a bit of a loner. Mixing with women of lower grades than yourself can mean that you are not taken seriously by male colleagues.

A clear emphasis on the need for self-determination and integrity as the most essential characteristics of professional life shines through a number of pieces of advice:

It's important to be oneself, even if that causes problems. It's also important to be professionally trained.

Do what you want to do and don't feel you have to conform.

My advice to young women would be to remember that you're an individual. Forget the barriers and go for it.

Even though I've sometimes been let down by believing that other people are honest and straightforward, I think that I would still want to persuade girls of the fundamental need to have integrity in all one's work.

Integrity also emerges as a strong theme in our interviewees' assessments of the qualities which they most like and admire in other women:

> I admire women who work conscientiously and achieve results — women who are independent, have self-respect and don't play games with you.

> I like extrovert, humorous women who are good at public speaking, and people of integrity.

> I like women who are honest and have a sense of humour.

> I admire women who do things in their own way and women who are self confident.

One form which such integrity assumes amongst several of our interviewees is that of caring for other people:

> Women should make sure that they make their own decisions. They should keep their integrity and be caring towards other people . . . Young women cannot afford to become complacent; there is still a struggle.

> I admire women who have the courage of their convictions and who will go out and do something about things. It's often more difficult for a woman to do this than a man. I also admire women who have done something positive to help other women. I admire Marie Stopes, for example, because birth control has done so much to liberate women.

But our interviewees also acknowledge that even the best of career strategies and the most outstanding qualities of integrity will sometimes be insufficient, that success is likely to be hard won, and that difficult choices may have to be made:

> I'd also want to point out to both boys and girls that life is not fair. I think I've led a very idealistic young life — I always used to think that justice would always prevail in the end, and that the best person would always get the job. I don't think that is necessarily true. It's not enough just to do a job well.

> You must be prepared to work hard and to be tough and determined, especially in a male dominated career.

> You have to be fairly tenacious and face up to prejudices, especially in male-dominated careers. You have to work hard and to be determined to make it. A sense of humour is important as well.

> My advice to girls is to get qualified. It's right to have your own aims and ambitions. Women can probably have everything they want in their lives, but perhaps not at the same time.

Our interviewees' descriptions of the kind of women whom they admire and like also often refer to the need to persevere despite obstacles:

I admire women who have come through adversity and also women who are not afraid to speak out.

I admire women who have struggled and eccentric women.

I admire women who can rise above the slings and arrows of their own fortune.

I most admire women who are good at what they do and who have worked their way up despite problems.

As we have already noted, such qualities are, of course, ones that also characterise our interviewees themselves. Are they then purely self regarding? Do they feel any sense of responsibility towards other women? How far are their declared statements of respect for women who have integrity and who struggle reflected in their own support of other women? We shall see in the following sections.

Looking at other women

Before considering the complex attitudes of our interviewees towards supporting other women, it is worth pausing for a little to examine the characteristics which they say they dislike in other women, as well as looking in more detail at those which they say they admire. As we shall see later in the discussion of attitudes towards the women's movement, when interviewees were asked about what kind of women they dislike, nearly all of those who say that they are anti-feminist, report that they dislike women whom they characterise as strident feminists. Those interviewees who are not so adamantly opposed to feminism or the women's movement tend to identify one major characteristic which they dislike in other women — dependence.

As we have noted in earlier chapters, our interviewees are themselves strikingly independent, and have often been so since childhood. As they see it, dependence in other women assume a variety of forms. In the first place, it is concerned with following the rules and becoming immersed in detail at the expense of larger issues:

I dislike petty minded women concerned with minutiae.

I hate women who are petty and rule-governed.

Secondly, dependence, as our interviewees depict it, consists of lack of understanding or awareness:

> I dislike women who are naive.

Most frequently, however, our interviewees speak of dependence on men as the characteristic which they dislike most in other women:

> I dislike women who are totally subservient to men. There are quite a few wives [where I work] who fall into that category.

> I dislike doormat women and battered women. There are so many opportunities given now for battered women to leave their husbands. Very often they choose to stay and have themselves to blame for what happens.

Associated with such dependence on men is the equally disliked characteristic of women's adopting male views of them as sexual objects:

> I dislike women who flaunt their sexuality.

> I dislike intensely women who use their feminine attractiveness as a means of career advancement; that seems to me a form of cheating.

  Strongly contrasted to these highly gender-specific characteristics of women whom our interviewees dislike are the relatively gender-neutral characteristics of those whom they most admire. We have already noted earlier in this chapter how much our interviewees admire integrity, independence, perseverance and hard work in other women. Their other replies to our question about what kind of women they most admire mention additional characteristics likely to be effective in professionals of either sex:

> I admire women who are committed to improving other people's lives. I particularly admire women who are good leaders and managers in the public sector.

> I like to see competent and capable women who don't rub your nose in their abilities. I admire women who can keep cool but manage to get things done.

> One woman whom I greatly admire is the Queen. I like intelligent, competent women who do what they say they can do.

> One of my greatest rôle models has been Winnie Ewing, MEP . . . I admire women with vision.

> I like women of courage, with sensitivity, humour and perseverance.

I admire women who are effective and women who can cope.

I like women who have a sense of their own self worth but not their own self importance.

I admire women who get up and go.

The theme of androgyny thus recurs. Those qualities which our interviewees admire and like in other women — such as integrity, perseverance, competence and leadership — are largely gender-neutral. Interviewees' dislikes, on the other hand, appear to be primarily gender-linked. If they do not actually dislike 'strident feminists', they tend at least to dislike women who are dependent on men. We had suggested in Chapter 5 that the professional and managerial styles of our interviewees appear to be androgynous. Now, in their attitudes towards other women, there appears to be an endorsement of gender-neutral or cross-gender characteristics in their likes, combined with a clear rejection of gender stereotypes expressed through their dislikes. Indeed, a number of interviewees emphasise that they admire people rather than women:

I admire mainly people rather than women specifically.

I admire both men and women, almost always for the same qualities in each.

As we shall see further below, this strong preference for androgyny also appears to play a part in the complex atittudes which our interviewees express about supporting other women. Nevertheless, it is important to note that a few interviewees do express admiration of characteristics which relate directly to gender. In particular, three interviewees without children express admiration of women who manage to combine having children with having a career:

I admire women who can have successful careers and raise well-balanced children. I know very few women who have managed to do this.

I admire women who have managed to have both a family and a career. (same quote from two interviewees)

It is noticeable, however, that these three mentions of admired female characteristics are all in the context of working women; none of our interviewees expresses admiration for, say, women just as mothers or as wives. Given this cluster of attitudes in which they tend to dislike predominatly female characteristics and to admire gender-neutral qualities in both men and women, how do our interviewees feel about supporting other women? Do they feel any responsibility towards other women? Is any support which they might offer restricted to like-minded professionals? To what extent do they take part in all female groups? In the following section we shall examine the effect of our interviewees' generally androgynous attitudes on their relationships with other women.

Supporting other women

There are, of course, many different forms in which women might be depicted as supporting other women: the more obvious possibilities include deliberately fostering other women at work, joining all female groups, networking with other women, and working for political change in areas in which women are perceived to be disadvantaged. All of these possibilities are reflected in the working and private lives of many of our interviewees. Because of the centrality of feminism and the women's movement during the major part of the working lives of most of our interviewees, their attitudes towards feminism, or the women's movement, will be our starting point for analysis.

Before analysing the replies to our questions about supporting other women, however, we should like to strike a note of caution. This study was not intended primarily as an examination of attitudes towards other women and the interviews did not attempt to define concepts such as feminism or the women's movement. The discussion which follows is therefore based on terms which are used generally rather than on precise definitions. The results are, at times, conceptually problematic. It is noticeable, for instance, that the terms feminism and the women's movement have very different meanings to many of our interviewees. Indeed, at times some interviewees claim to reject their concept of feminism while clearly adhering in practice to what are often seen as major tenets of the women's movement. It was, however, simply not possible to define terms with any degree of rigour during the course of the relatively brief but widely ranging interviews.

Depending on the perspective and interpretation used, our interviewees, as women who have succeeded in posts previously occupied primarily by men, could be seen as exemplars of feminism because they have achieved equal opportunities in their own professional lives or as betrayers of the collectivist principles of feminism because they have apparently sought their own career development rather than working together with their sisters for mutual help. It is thus not surprising that their attitudes towards feminism tend to be ambivalent.

Just over half of our interviewees for which such information is available say that they support the women's movement with varying degrees of reservation, while over a quarter reject it:

Cartoon by Jacky Fleming

Figure 31

BELIEF IN THE WOMEN'S MOVEMENT

	%
No	28
Yes	2
Yes, with Reservations	54
Not Known	16

No. of Interviewees = 50

When asked about their attitudes to the women's movement, many interviewees express explicit ambivalence:

> 'My views on the women's movement are, at best, ambivalent. I found the movement vaguely embarrassing. Women can make it if they are strong and determined; women who don't get to the top don't deserve to be or don't choose to be.

> The women's movement has been necessary, although in some ways it was hysterical.

> I'm turned off by all-female groups; I am not a joiner of networks . . . I am a sceptical feminist. You can't be a woman in this day and age without being a feminist of some sort: there has been systematic discrimination against women. I hope that in the future this will slowly disappear.

In particular, interviewees object to what they see as the exclusion of men from the women's movement:

> I've always felt uneasy about radical feminism — its wholesale rejection of the male world has always seemed both suspect and ineffective. But I would certainly call myself a feminist — even if I might tone down some of my views depending on the context in which I was expressing them!

> I have never been involved in the women's movement. I believe that it is much more important to educate the men rather than the women, although I do see the need for women to be supported by, for example, single-sex training courses.

> I'm not a really strong feminist. I think everyone should be treated the same.

> The women's movement was very useful at the time, but many of the problems face men as well as women. It's really time to look at both genders.

> The women's movement has helped in some ways but hindered in others. *Everyone* has rights.

Most frequently, the women's movement is valued for its effectiveness in raising issues and starting to change attitudes, although often at a price:

> The women's movement, apart from the lunatic fringe, has helped. It has raised awareness, and it does help to change attitudes.

> I'm ambivalent about the women's movement. It has caused an awareness of women's issues, but it has also caused antagonism.

> I'm a member of several all-women's groups, including the Scottish Convention of Women, but I was not active in the women's movement. Many of the attitudes of the women's movement were very restrictive — you had to wear a head scarf and carry a basket! Issues, however, did have to be raised, and the women's movement did that. Unfortunately, the trail blazers alienated a lot of men and women.

Probably the most common judgement amongst those who do support the movement with reservations is that:

> The women's movement has both helped and hindered.

Amongst those who fell into the category of being 'sceptical feminists' (the term is Richard's, 1980), there is a general feeling of responsibility for other women, albeit a responsibility which assumes many different forms:

I feel I have a responsibility and a duty to help other women, although I'm not a member of any all-women's groups.

I became a feminist only when I began work. I've been a member of various all-women groups, for example, the Scottish Convention of Women. I don't believe that I personally can be responsible for other women but I do have a deep commitment to helping them to develop their own careers. I feel that it's important for women to be members of a trade union. Supporting other women is important to me. I'm willing to talk to any young female [in my own profession] who wants help. I feel that on an individual basis such help can very worth while.

I've never had any strong relationship with the women's movement and have not been active in feminism until recently. I could see some benefits from the movement, but never felt strongly the need to join it . . . I do feel responsibility towards both practical and theoretical issues regarding other women in [my institution and another organisation] . . . I could see myself becoming active on the issue of child benefit, because I feel very strongly that it affects all women generally.

I'm not a member of any all female groups, by choice. I hadn't thought of being a role model for other women until quite recently. I'm not sure how much I could help other women on the career ladder, but I'm certainly interested in trying to.

This desire to support other women is also strong in the one interviewee who has taken part in the women's movement:

I do feel responsible towards other women . . . I was actively involved in the women's movement in the seventies.

Of the 28 per cent of interviewees who reject the women's movement, probably the major source of rejection is the dislike of what they perceive as strident feminists:

I don't admire strident feminists . . . and I dislike women who let other women down.

I'm not convinced that the women's movement has been a great deal of help to women. Women should have the strength of character just to be women. I don't like strident feminists. It's quite sad if women have no time to be at home.

I don't like women who grouse about women's lot and women who think the world owes them a living.

I don't like whingeing women and I don't like absolute feminists.

I dislike pretentiousness . . . I dislike ultra feminists, who are usually humourless.

I hate strident feminists. If anything has put [male members of my profession] off females, it would be the loud-mouthed feminists who occasionally appear on the . . . scene. They just do not gain any respect from their colleagues and put the woman's cause back rather than forward.

I dislike women's libbers who get away with behaviour which wouldn't be tolerated in men.

I dislike women who dislike men.

Indeed, the two major characteristics of feminism identified by those of our interviewees who reject it are that it is embittered and embarrassing. One interviewee, however, rejects feminism on the grounds of the greater importance of the class struggle:

Feminism is predominantly a middle-class movement. The lot of women is not really going to improve until the class system is broken down in this country.

Paralleling to some extent this diversity of their attitudes towards feminism, our interviewees fall into a number of different categories in their attitudes towards being and working with groups composed entirely of women. In the first place, 38 per cent of interviewees express explicit dislike of being with all-women groups:

I don't like all-female groups, don't like being with all women — I avoid them if at all possible. I also don't like being with women with children. Maybe it's because I don't have any of my own. Maybe it's because I don't have much in common with them.

I have never sought out all women groups and feel slightly ambivalent about them.

Although I have children, I have never liked meeting together with other women just on the grounds that they are women. I hate the division at parties in Scotland whereby men and women talk mainly with their own sex. I simply have much more in common with people with whom I share professional interests or wider political and social concerns than with women just because were are of the same sex. I really dislike things such as women's coffee mornings and tea parties.

I'm much more interested in what make men tick. I don't like all women's groups and avoid them whenever possible.

But 40 per cent of interviewees express either tolerance of, or active preference for, being and working in all-female groups:

> I am a member of a number of all-women's groups . . . I enjoy working with women and being with them on a social level as well.

> Issues can appear to be women's issues, but very often they are human issues. If it is not appropriate for women, it is not appropriate. It is important to value being a woman and to value other women. A lot of good things are happening, but many are invisible — women's networks can highlight issues.

A number of interviewees mention being members of formally constituted women's organations with specific aims, such as the Scottish Convention of Women:

> A watershed in my life was the day I found out about, and eventually joined, the Scottish Convention of Women . . . I'm very supportive of women's groups. SCOW has an important role to play in Scotland.

Other interviewees mention groups of like-minded professional women such as the Soroptomists, Business and Professional Women and the Women's Engineering Society. A few of those who express a liking for all-female groups mention informal groupings of women at their own level or sharing their own professional interests:

> I don't have any direct involvement in the women's movement, but I do feel that female networks can be very useful . . . I find it difficult to meet and talk with women at the same level as I am in Scotland, but there is a small group of other women directors whom I meet fairly regularly.

> It was when I was appointed [to a senior post] that I realised I was a closet feminist, when I saw, especially amongst ethnic minorities, just how poorly females were treated in many sections of society. Now I'm keen on women's networks and have been very involved in [one of my profession].

Most often, interviewees who express a liking (though rarely an exclusive liking) for meeting in all-female groups refer to their membership of Network, which describes itself as 'a forum in which successful women can develop professional and social contacts [and] . . . ensure that women's contribution and influence is (*sic*) recognised as a vital force in all the corridors of power, be they in the professions, industry or the arts.' (Network mission statement) Twelve out of our interviewees are, or have been, members of Network in Scotland. Most of them express positive support for it as a concept:

I helped to found a branch of Network. Women shoud work together and help each other get on.

I joined Network at its inception. I've never suffered direct sexual discrimination or harrassment, but I feel that an organisation like Network has been a life saver.

I'm a member of Network. Organisations such as it can do a lot to encourage women in career development.

The motivation for joining an organisation such as Network, however, is rarely simply to help other women, as one interviewee makes explicit:

I joined Network in order to form female contacts in business, rather than to mentor other women.

Regardless of whether they make use of female networks or not, most of our interviewees appear to prefer mixing with both male and female fellow professionals:

I've been asked to join several women's groups but so far have not — mainly by choice. I'm a member of the local Chamber of Commerce and find that very useful for networking locally.

I was a member of Network briefly, but I prefer mixed groups of fellow professionals.

I actually like networking both in all-female professional groups as well as in mixed groups. It seems to me that they each serve different purposes and so are each valuable in their own ways. If I had to choose between them, however, I'd unquestionably go for mixed sex networking; amongst other considerations, there aren't very many other senior women in [my own field] with whom I could network!

Professional women are starting to get together more, but I feel ambivalent about all-women groups. Networking is crucial in any career development. But I've found it much more useful to network in a mixed professional group rather than in a single sex women's group.

Here again the theme of androgyny recurs. But how far do our interviewees feel that mixed-sex groupings and gender-neutral qualities offer possibilities for the future of women in Scotland? Does legislation have a role to play? What else might help to further women's career development? We shall now consider our interviewees' responses to these issues.

Legislation

As we shall see in the next section, our interviewees on the whole are optimistic about the future for professional women in Scotland, despite their accounts of the difficulties which they have encountered in their own career development and despite their generally held belief that conditions for senior women are harsher in Scotland than elsewhere in Europe or in North America. For over half of our interviewees, more effective legislation relating to factors in women's career development is desirable as a way to reach that better future.

Figure 32

BELIEF IN THE VALUE OF LEGISLATION

	%
Yes	58
With Reservations	6
No	4
Not Known	32

No. of Interviewees = 50

Of those who believe that legislation does help to promote more effective equal opportunities for women, several are highly enthusiastic about its likely effect:

Legislation is the beginning of changing society.

Legislation does help, and further legislation would help further.

Legislation is important, it does help. Women couldn't do it all on their own.

As we have seen in Chapters 4 and 5, the presence of children is a major factor in women's career development in Scotland. A number of interviewees therefore emphasise the need for better child care legislation:

I strongly believe that laws do help. I would like to see more family law and laws for better child care facilities.

More child care legislation should be introduced.

There should be more legislation. There should be tax rebates on paid domestic help and many more local authority nursery places for people like me; I'm not in favour of work-based crèches.

Legislation does help to change — it gives a framework on which to build. I also believe that there should be more child care legislation.

Another focus lies on fairer and more effective equal opportunities provision:

I am a firm believer in legislation. The problem about the ineffectiveness of much current equal opportunities legislation in the UK is not that it is the law but the kind of legislation that it is; the need to prove each case of sex discrimination rather than have class actions means that most cases just don't get brought forward in the first place. I'm especially hopeful about the impact which I hope the European Community will have on our equal opportunities legislation in the future.

More and better sex discrimination legislation should be brought in. Legislation, I believe very strongly, does change attitudes.

Legislation is crucial. I know people say it doesn't change attitudes, but there are examples of how legislation does change them, as in drinking and driving. Legislation is needed to support child care and the caring side of people's lives generally. And the tax and pension systems need to be looked at. I've paid all this money into [an institutional] pension scheme but if I die [my husband] won't get a penny. I just think that's grossly unfair.

Most of those who support the need for legislation, however, feel that, although it is necessary, it will not in itself be sufficient to improve opportunities for women:

I think a legal framework is important. In the long term, however, attitudes are also important and have to be changed.

Women themselves have to change things. Legislation can only help partly in changing attitudes. Women must have their self-confidence built in order to be able to put forward their views and their demands, in a clear and articulate way.

I'm wary about how far legislation can change attitudes, but existing legislation has helped.

Barriers do exist. One important thing is to build up women's confidence. Many of the barriers facing women start to build up from primary school level. Legislation does help — by making people aware of problems.

One interviewee is conscious of potential conflict between the desirability of legislation for women and its undesirable effect on their employers:

> I'm not sure if more legislation would help. More protection might be good
> for women but it would be very difficult for companies.

One interviewee believes that legislation is simply unnecessary:

> Women's opportunities will evolve naturally. Legislation would do little to
> change things.

Because we do not have any information about how sixteen interviewees feel about the role of legislation, it is impossible to conclude that our interviewees overwhelmingly support the idea that further legislation is needed to improve equal opportunities for women. It is nevertheless striking that a very substantial majority of those for whom we do have information support the idea that legislation is a necessary, if not a sufficient, means of bringing about change for the better of women. Analysis of the political backgrounds of those who support the idea of legislation shows that such support extends across the political spectrum, although socialists and nationalists tend to believe to a greater extent than conservatives in the efficiency of the legislative process in bringing about social change.

Vision of the future

Despite their belief in the efficacy of legislation, the optimism about the future which is expressed by most interviewees does not appear to rest on whether relevant legislation might actually be enacted. Rather, interviewees tend to believe that change is occurring in any case even without legislative intervention. In particular, having identified male attitudes as a major barrier to women's career development, many interviewees believe that it is precisely in such attitudes that change is taking place:

> Present male attitudes are not only outdated but are wasteful of women's
> talents. I do believe that attitudes are changing slowly.

> The main barrier to women's career development in Scotland is its culture.
> Things *are* changing, and younger men are much more broad-minded.
> There are also major changes in the expectations of younger women.

> Organisations vary enormously in their attitude towards women. But
> hurdles do exist. I hope it's a generational thing. Attitudes *are* changing,
> especially amongst younger men.

Many interviewees believe that women themselves, at a time when demographic trends and political changes may help their career development, will bring about more favourable conditions for more senior women. In the first place, several interviewees believe that particular professions will offer excellent opportunities for women. A few interviewees spontaneously recommend their own professions to other women, especially law, computing, the ministry, and, in the long-term, surveying. Secondly, interviewees believe that increased numbers of women in senior position may in themselves help to create a more favourable climate:

> I don't really think that one or two women at the top of organisations will make all that much difference, partly because so much depends on their attitude towards other women, partly because so few are not likely to have any significant effect. The real differences will occur as more and more women come through the system; once there is a critical mass of them, then things will start to change.

> I think things are improving in [my profession]. We now have a training manager and two other senior women in [my company]

Thirdly, a number of interviewees believe that, as one of them phrases it, 'Barriers will be forced to disappear because of demographic trends.'

Because of this emphasis on the role of demographic trends, interviewees see the next ten years or so as crucial:

> I'm enthusiastic and optimistic about women's future. I'm not so sure who said it, but there's nothing as powerful as an idea whose time has come. Women *must* make it in the next five to ten years . . . Politics will change things, especially if a Scottish Assembly is set up. I'm very much in favour of empowering the individual. I want to change the way we all are in Scotland.

> I am very cautiously optimistic. Things may change slowly in the next ten to fifteen years.

> What worries me about the current fashion for speaking about how the demographic downturn will benefit women in employment are two things. First, although employers will have to make employment more attractive and more accessible for women, once the downturn starts to move upward again at the end of the nineties, employers will be likely to turn off all the special arrangements that they turned on in the early nineties unless both men and women have found them to be to their advantage. And I'm not clear how the decrease in school leavers will in itself benefit women's careers: there is never likely to be a shortage of male applicants for top jobs!'

At the same time, too, several interviewees are less hopeful that change will automatically mean that men and women eventually achieve equality:

> There are definitely still barriers in Scotland. Things have changed and
> improved. But women may reach a ceiling. I doubt whether there will ever
> be total parity between men and women.

Other interviewees are highly conscious of what they see as the barriers
for women in their own professions; medicine and the academic world are
both cited as fields in which discrimination against women is still widely
practised. Moreover, the optimism of some interviewees appears to be
based on a belief that one must be optimistic rather than on any very sure
sense of the certainty of positive change:

> The best way to change society is by example. Screamers normally become
> martyrs. You must be optimistic and positive about the future.

Conclusion

We thus leave our interviewees in the midst of a cautious optimism about
the future for women like them in Scotland. On the whole, our younger
interviewees are more optimistic, and our older ones rather more
pessimistic about the outcomes in the twenty-first century. In the next
chapter we shall consider how far such views of the future appear to be
supported by currently available evidence and how more women could
play a fuller role in their society.

Conclusion

Our analysis of the professional and personal experiences, characteristics and strategies of senior women in Scotland points to a number of factors in common in their lives which appear to have contributed towards their success. The investigation also raises crucial issues to be addressed by all those who believe — whether for reasons of economic efficiency or in the interests of a fairer society — that women can make a more substantial contribution to the life of Scotland than they have yet been able to achieve. Most of this chapter considers these factors and issues. The chapter also takes account of apparent changes in Scottish public life during the period in which we have been writing the book and suggests a range of indicators which are likely to characterise the future for senior women in Scotland.

Factors in success

In their professional experience, our interviewees tend to be exceptions to the general expectation that it is primarily men who occupy senior posts in Scotland. As we noted in Chapter 1, the overall participation rate of females in senior positions across a wide range of professional fields in Scotland ranges from 0 to 5 per cent. Virtually all of our interviewees are, or were, the most senior women in their organisation, and most of them are the first women to have occupied such a senior position. They have therefore arrived at their positions in great contrast to the past and current experience of most women in Scotland. They have had to counter those Scottish historical patterns, social attitudes and employment practices which have all assumed male hegemony, and, on the whole, most of them have done so in a climate of opinion which did not recognise gender as an important issue.

In particular, the women whom we interviewed have achieved their positions despite a number of factors which could reasonably have been expected to deter them. These barriers include:

● restrictive attitudes of both men and women towards women aiming for, and occupying, senior positions
● informal selection methods favouring males in recruitment and promotion
● the possibility of age discrimination, which restricts opportunities for women returning to the labour market after child rearing
● partners' geographical mobility
● the lack of good quality, affordable child care
● the apparent ineffectiveness of equal opportunities policies in most workplaces.

A number of characteristics and strategies appear to have countered the adverse effects of these factors. In the first place, our interviewees' early experiences at home appear to have laid the foundation for later achievement in professional life. Interviewees' family backgrounds were characterised by:

● early development of organising abilities
● mothers who worked outside the home in paid or voluntary employment
● commitment to religious or political causes.

Above all, most of our interviewees' families placed substantial emphasis on education and the achievement of academic qualifications. This strategy appears to have been particularly important in shaping interviewees' high level of participation in both higher education and continuing professional education. As learners, interviewees are characterised by:

● an exceptionally high level of educational achievement, usually (but not invariably) supported by parents
● for those who were mature students, a focus on professionally relevant qualifications
● commitment to continuing education, particularly at management level
● emphasis on, and excellence in, performance-related activities.

As they move into paid employment, interviewees' career strategies have much in common with each other:

● initial experimentation with types of jobs and employers
● tapestried careers, creating a pattern from related areas of work
● emphasis on innovation and change, including a tendency to make major career moves every four to seven years
● some use of mentors, usually of both sexes
● reluctance to seek legal redress for problems of sex discrimination or harassment
● hard work, usually over long hours
● careful attention to personal image.

Within their own workplaces, interviewees' strategies also tend to share a number of common elements:

● emphasis on long-term strategic thinking, flexibility of approach, challenges to suspect methods and ideas, firm fair action, and team work
● androgynous or gender-neutral management styles
● preference for working with both men and women
● some commitment to equal opportunities policies and practices.

In combining their personal and professional lives, too, our interviewees share many similar characteristics:

● belief in the need for balance
● high level of awareness of the difficulty of combining a serious career with the care of young children
● commitment to a high level of activity in a wide range of leisure interests and voluntary work
● some imaginative attempts to solve adverse effects of partners' geographical mobility.

Overall, perhaps the most crucial factor, which appears to run through nearly all of the interviews, is a general, realistic recognition of success as hard won, with difficult choices to be made. A number of our interviewees refer spontaneously to the need to demolish the myth of the superwoman, who has, and can do, everything.

Despite these common patterns in the strategies adopted by our interviewees, however, they are far from forming a uniform model of successful women. To begin with, as our analysis has suggested throughout the book, there is often quite substantial divergence from the overall patterns. Despite the general picture depicted above, for instance, a few of our interviewees were not committed to any causes when young, while by no means all of them had working mothers. One fifth of our interviewees did not proceed directly to higher education, and, indeed, two of them have never acquired higher education qualifications. Rather than changing jobs every four to seven years, a number of interviewees have remained with the same employer throughout most of their working lives, while others have changed jobs frequently. A very few actively prefer working only with women, while several others appear to have internalised 'male' management styles.

Generally, however, most of our interviewees share most strategies in common. Those individuals who are exceptions to any one strategy or characteristic are never consistently divergent from other senior women. For example, an interviewee who, unusually, entered employment directly after school will nevertheless tend to share others' androgynous management styles. Similarly, the minority who have chosen to remain single tend to prefer working with both men and women in the same way as their married counterparts.

Nevertheless, in two important respects, our interviewees are not 'strategic' women at all. Firstly, their lives tend to contain unresolved, conflicting demands, and stress features significantly for many of them. The major causes of perceived conflict are all connected with the relationship between professional and personal life:

1.   Women's successful careers tend to be linked with remaining single or having a partner who is highly supportive or breaking up their marriage; the main reasons mentioned for marital breakdown are divergence between male and female career progression and women's dislike of domesticity contrasted with their husbands' preference for traditional households.

2.   For dual-career families, there is often serious divergence between the geographical demands of each partner's career, with the husband's career moves tending to take precedence over the wife's except where dual site arrangements are made.

3.   For single parents, the demands of a career, children and housework invariably exceed the time available; such mothers are under serious pressure while children are growing up.

Secondly, nearly all of our interviewees view the development of their own careers as primarily fortuitous rather than strategic. Although their advice to young women emphasises the need to plan careers, most of our interviewees have not practised what they now advocate. Instead, their accounts of their own careers depict unexpected opportunities which they seized and fortunate occurences which they developed to advantage. With a few exceptions, our general impression is one of women who accept that they cannot fully control their own lives — mainly because of their actual or potential relationship with partners or children, whose requirements in the last analysis will be placed first. The major source of continuing conflict in the lives of those who have been, or are, married is unquestionably the tension between the demands of domestic and professional life.

Despite this conflict, however, most of our interviewees say that they are happy with their lives. To some extent, it may be that they have after all developed a strategy for dealing with unresolved conflict by simply accepting it. They manage to contain the more extreme forms of conflict while also trying to give each of the many elements in their lives a due share of attention. The results are sometimes messy, such as dual-site marriages or the expenditure of more money than they can really afford on good quality child care. In other cases, the cause of what is perceived as serious potential conflict is simply avoided, as it is by those interviewees who told us that they do not wish to marry or to have children.

But what do these strategies and conflicts imply for women who have tried but failed to reach similar positions? What do they imply for women who have decided not to compete in what they regard as male positions? And what implications do they have for the way in which working life will be organised in the 1990s? We shall now consider these and other issues arising from our findings.

Issues

Our interviewees have raised a number of further questions for us about the employment experiences of women in Scotland. We are not rashly proposing to try to answer these questions here, because they are, almost invariably, questions which need to be addressed by further research. Instead, we shall outline the rationale for our concern about the issues of education and careers guidance, the allocation of domestic responsibilities, the gender composition of holders of senior posts, the recognition of gender as an issue in education and employment, and the effects of current legislation on equal opportunities.

EDUCATION AND CAREERS GUIDANCE
Nearly all of our interviewees report that they had little or no guidance at school about possible careers and that they embarked on higher education often without any clear sense of their real intellectual and vocational interests. Although several report pre- or post-graduation interviews with

university careers services, it appears that very few left university with
any clear idea of the range of professional careers available to them. As
Nelson (1989) has shown, the more education individuals in Scotland
have, the more likely they are to have sought and received guidance about
vocational education and training opportunities and about employment. If
our highly educated interviewees experienced such a lack of guidance,
therefore, it is likely that less qualified girls and women will have received
even less.

Since the time when our interviewees were at school, a system of
careers guidance in schools and, to a more limited extent, for adults, has
been developed. A number of important questions now arise:

1.   To what extent have the career expectations of girls and young
women changed as a result of them receiving educational and vocational
guidance?

2.   How far are girls and women aware of the full range of careers
options?

3.   Are girls and women being positively encouraged to consider those
types of education, training and work which in Scotland remain
predominantly male dominated?

4.   How far are both sexes who make non-traditional choices supported
by accurate assessments of the barriers and strategies for success in
different non-traditional fields?

5.   In what ways do assumptions about appropriate employment for
working-class girls and women share the careers guidance which they
receive?

6.   To what extent does the training of careers guidance staff include
gender awareness?

7.   How far are careers guidance staff knowledgeable about programmes
in other European countries to promote diversification of occupational
choice?

As far as we know, the relative lack of public or private funding for
gender-related research in Scotland has meant that, so far, little evidence
is available to begin to answer such questions in any depth.

THE ALLOCATION OF DOMESTIC RESPONSIBILITIES

Our interviewees report three major areas of domestic responsibility:
housework, the care of elderly relatives and child care. Although all three
of these areas are inter-related — partly because all of them tend to take
place at home — we shall consider each of them in turn because each
tends to have affected our interviewees in different ways.

Whether married or single, nearly all of our interviewees undertake a substantial amount of responsibility for *housework* — with the exception of one woman whose mother and partner look after all the domestic work. Those women who are both single and childless, and who are therefore likely not to have exceptionally heavy burdens of housework, barely touch on the subject at all during the interviews, although several mention that they employ domestic help of various kinds, ranging from cleaners to caterers. For those who had been married but are now single, disagreement between former husband and wife about housework appears to be a factor in marital breakdown, with men tending to prefer (or to insist) that their full-time employed wives should nevertheless undertake almost the entire burden of housework.

For our childless married interviewees, the demands of housework vary considerably, as do their ways of managing it. Several of our interviewees report that their husbands share half or more of housework. Many more report that, as wives, they undertake the major share of the work, despite verbally supportive husbands. As do single interviewees, childless married interviewees often report employing domestic help, including gardeners.

For our married interviewees with children, the demands of housework are, of course, heavier than those in childless households, and such interviewees are more likely to view housework as an issue in their lives. As might be expected from national UK findings (see, for example, *Social Trends*, 1989), our interviewees tend to report that husbands provide more substantial verbal than practical support, with more male attention being given to child care than to housework. Here again, there appears to be considerable employment of domestic help. In only one case does a married interviewee report that she has carried the full domestic burden on her own throughout her life as a full-time mature student and subsequently in a full time professional career.

Our single interviewees with children found, understandably, the greatest difficulty in getting sufficient help with housework, at least while children were young. Although such households may have a lower income than the normally two income households of married interviewees, our interviewees who are single mothers report a particularly high use of employed domestic help while their children were young.

For other women who work full time but who have not aspired to, or reached, senior posts, the solutions of paid domestic help often used by our interviewees are, of course, likely to be available only where families have a substantial income. Otherwise, the allocation of housework amongst the members of a household remains a major issue. As *Social Trends* (1989) shows, even in households where the woman works full-time outside the home, household tasks are not shared equally: where both partners work full time, in 72 per cent of households housework is still done mainly by women; it is shared equally only in 22 per cent. Women who work part time, however, carry almost as heavy a domestic burden as women who do not work outside the home at all. *Social Trends* also shows that, in their attitudes towards whether tasks should be shared equally, full-time married women are 'much more egalitarian' than their male partners.

In practice, then, the domestic lives of married women who are employed full-time in Scotland remain much more demanding than those of married men. This circumstance in itself is likely to create disadvantages for women who aspire to senior positions as well for others who simply prefer to be employed outside the home but who are not interested in pursuing serious careers. How long are such disadvantages likely to persist? One major issue in the future is likely to be the expectations of boys and girls about their own future domestic respnsibilities. A number of questions arise:

1.   How far do young men and women in Scotland in the 1990s believe that housework is a joint responsibility of all those who are old enough to undertake it?
2.   How far are boys and young men currently trained to do housework?
3.   Is the apparent discrepancy between male verbal and practical support for working females diminishing?

A second important demand in the domestic lives of some of our interviewees is the need to care for *elderly relatives*, either at home or by frequent visits. It appears that such responsibilities are assumed willingly and fully by both married and single interviewees, although those who care for elderly relatives comment on the time and often the stress involved in doing so. Because our interviewees work, or have worked, predominantly full-time, however, none of our interviewees cares full-time for an elderly relative.

At a time when the numbers of very old people in the community are increasing rapidly, our interviewees do not share the particularly difficult circumstances of those who provide such caring full-time. The very fact of their not sharing these circumstances, however, raises a number of questions about those women who have not been able to undertake full-time employment or to embark on serious careers because of their responsibility for elderly relatives:

1.   What is the education and training background of those who are full-time carers?

2. How far have the carers of those who provide full-time care been disrupted or ended by such caring?

3. To what extent have assessments been made of the educational potential of elderly people in Scotland, both to enable them to lead more fulfilling lives and to relieve the burden of their carers?

By far the most significant domestic issue in the lives of just under half of our interviewees, however, is that of *children*. There is considerable doubt amongst our interviewees about whether it is possible to resolve an apparently irreconcilable conflict between providing good quality child care and having a serious career. It is primarily for this reason that many of our married interviewees have deliberately chosen to remain childless. It is not by chance that over half of our interviewees are childless by choice: about half of able female school leavers in Scotland either agree with, or are uncertain about, a statement that 'it is rare for a woman to combine a career and a family and make a success of both.' (Burnhill and McPherson, 1984).

The difficulties of combining children and a serious career may also be reflected in the fact that those of our interviewees who are parents have chosen very diverse ways of trying to combine both. To begin with, the variable in which our interviewees who are mothers are most unlike one another is that of child care, where substantial numbers have chosen, variously, full-time career breaks, part-time career breaks or continuous full-time employment. The difficulty of combining child care and careers is also reflected in the fact that many of our interviewee mothers have each tried a number of different strategies to combine the two — perhaps starting with a part-time career break, then moving fairly quickly to full-time employment, or starting with a partial career break then moving rapidly into a full-time break. Thirdly, the difficulty is illustrated by the fact that those mothers who have remained in continuous full-time employment report a wide variety of child care arrangements, including female relatives, husbands, nannies, au pairs, child minders and private nurseries.

Our findings suggest that there is, indeed, a good chance that a conflict between young children and careers may be almost irreconcilable — given the present one level of provision of good quality, affordable child care in Scotland. Recent studies have suggested (Scott, 1989a; Mehuish and Moss, 1990) that what matters most for children is not where they are cared for — at home, in a nursery or with child minders — but whether the care is of sufficiently high quality. The widespread lack of high quality affordable child care in Scotland appears to mean that mothers without high incomes face a choice of caring for children themselves or using poor quality but affordable provision.

A related factor in the difficulty of combining children and careers is the biological clock, which ticks mercilessly for women embarking on careers. As we have just seen, good quality child care remains very expensive in Scotland. Women who aim for professional success, and the substantial income which success usually brings, before having children, have to take account of the awkward fact that women tend to be promoted later than men and may therefore not achieve such success until they are well into their forties; at this age first pregnancies — to say nothing of subsequent ones — are at best risky.

It is thus not surprising that more than half of our sample are childless. But it remains a matter for serious long-term concern that such a high proportion of able women are choosing not to bear children because of the particular conflict created by the present level of provision of child care in Britain. The lack of affordable high quality child care is also likely to be a major — if not even the major — factor in the lives of almost all mothers who decide that they would like to re-enter the labour market. A recent study in Scotland (Scott, 1989b) has found that two-thirds of women who are currently at home full-time with their pre-school children would prefer to be at work if suitable childcare were available.

Those mothers for whom private child care is too expensive tend to work part time; it is not surprising that the United Kingdom has one of the lowest proportions of publicly funded child care and the highest proportion of female part-time workers in the European Community (EC, 1989). The problem is that part-time jobs tend to be both low pay and low status, unlikely to lead to more substantial employment, much less to serious career development.

The need for affordable high quality child care is now well documented, although less evidence is available about the mix of provision required. The wide range of types of child care provision used by our mother interviewees may reflect not merely the difficulty of finding suitable high quality provision. To some extent, the variety appears also to reflect the fact that parental requirements are likely to vary. As we write this, however, political will to provide help with child care of almost any kind is not yet powerful in Britain, although the decision to pay child care allowances as part of the Employment Training programme is a significant step forward.

Despite the difficulties, the overwhelming fact remains that those of our interviewees who did decide to become mothers express primarily delight and joy in their children, and, as far as we can tell, the children themselves appear to thrive. Moreover, the intriguing fact remains that, even where they have taken (usually brief) full-time career breaks, the mothers in our interviewees do not otherwise appear to have careers which are significantly different from other senior women. Such women are in themselves proof that children can be combined with serious careers, but their paucity is also an indication of the sometimes extreme difficulty of doing so.

On this issue of child care, there appear to be fewer questions which remain to be addressed in future research. It is true that one might ask why the findings so far have been almost entirely ignored in central government policy-making, but that question lies outside the scope of our concerns here. The two remaining questions now appear to be:

1.   In what mix should various forms of high quality child care be made available?
2.   Since most mothers will be unable to pay the full cost of child care, who will subsidise it?

THE GENDER COMPOSITION OF HOLDERS OF SENIOR POSTS

As we have noted throughout this study, until very recently there has been a dearth of evidence about the gender composition of the holders of senior posts in Scotland. Studies are now beginning to accumulate, but evidence remains patchy, and it is difficult to obtain an overview of the situation across all the major professions. In the following section on 'Indicators', we shall glance at the evidence for changes that appear to be taking place in the representation of women in professional positions in Scotland. Meanwhile, if, as the figures so far available (supplemented by a wealth of anecdotal evidence) suggest, women are very significantly under-represented in senior posts, the following questions may need to be addressed for each professional grouping:

1.   What is the overall pattern for qualification for, and recruitment and promotion of, males and females in the profession?
2.   How have these patterns changed over the past ten years?
3.   For members and conveners of major committees and advisory bodies, what is the overall proportion of male and female?
4.   What are the attitudes of both sexes and of different age groupings within the profession to the moving of women into senior positions?
5.   How far is training in equal opportunities (gender) made available?
6.   In what way, and to what effect, are equal opportunities policies monitored and evaluated within the profession?

THE RECOGNITION OF GENDER AS AN ISSUE

Before such questions are likely to be addressed by researchers and policy-makers in Scotland, however, there needs to be greater recognition of gender both as an issue and as a variable in research into education and employment. As we shall see in more detail later in this chapter, such recognition is beginning to emerge in Scotland. Meanwhile, the implication of what our interviewees have told us is that, while they believe that gender has been a highly significant issue which tends negatively to have affected their own experience of employment, this belief is not yet widely shared by their employers. Judging from the experience reported by our interviewees, it appears that, where they do recognise gender as an issue, at least some Scottish employers do so by practising outright or subtle sex discrimination or harassment.

However true such a picture may have been of the past employment experiences cited by our interviewees, the future does appear to be rather more encouraging, as we shall see at the end of this chapter. Meanwhile, important questions remain to be addressed:

1.   How far do all publicly accessible statistics break down patterns for males and females at all levels of education, training and employment?
2.   How far does all research into education, training and employment differentiate between patterns for males and females and how far does it attempt to explore the reasons for any significant differences found?
3.   Why is considering gender a possible variable not an explicit recruitment of all publicly funded research in Scotland?

THE EFFECTS OF CURRENT LEGISLATION ON EQUAL OPPORTUNITIES

As far as we can tell, none of our interviewees has made personal use of the United Kingdom's equal opportunities legislation, despite the fact that a substantial number of them report their belief that they have experienced sexual harassment or discrimination. There appears to be a widespread belief that having recourse to such legislative provisions spells future career difficulty for the women who make use of it. How far this belief is founded on evidence has not yet, as far as we know, been tested in Scotland. The following questions remain to be answered:

1.   To what extent has equal opportunities legislation been used by women applying to, or in, different occupational groupings in Scotland?
2.   What are the outcomes of cases brought to industrial tribunals?
3.   What are the immediate and longer term effects on the employment lives of the women concerned?

As we have been suggesting throughout this section, important changes have been occurring on many of the issues considered here. In the following section we shall look at some of the available evidence for change and shall speculate on that basis about the future opportunities for women who aspire to senior positions in Scotland.

Indicators for the Future

At the beginning of the 1990s in Scotland, many of the trends for women in senior positions are positive. Increasing numbers and proportions of women are acquiring qualifications in higher education. Increasing numbers and proportions of women are entering professional occupations. It appears as if slightly increased numbers of women are being appointed to senior positions. Moreover, there has been substantial development in the awareness of gender as an issue in Scottish life.

Albeit from often very small numbers, the numbers and proportions of women in major professions in Scotland have grown steadily during the 1980s and are expected to continue to grow in the present decade (SCDI, 1988). We regret that it is not possible to chart this growth across all professions and in all sectors, partly because a number of United Kingdom or British bodies, such as the British Institute of Management, do not keep separate statistics for their Scottish membership. In addition, at the time of writing, some Scottish organisations do not yet have, or are unable to supply, a breakdown of their members or of the profession as a whole by gender.

For those professional bodies and other organisations from whom we have been able to collect data, the trend in female participation is invariably upward. The numbers of female members of the Institute of Chartered Accountants in Scotland grew from 5 per cent in 1981 to 11 per cent in 1990 (Institute of Chartered Accountants, 1990), while the Chartered Association of Certified Accountants' proportion of female members in Scotland rose from 3 per cent in 1970 to 10 per cent in 1990. In the Royal Institution of Chartered Surveyors in Scotland, women form only 3 per cent of corporate members in 1990, but 16 per cent of probationer and student members are female. Slater (1990) comments that 'while clearly some degree of caution needs to be applied to these latter figures, in as much as not all of these Student and Probationer members will proceed to full corporate status, the great majority can be expected to do so, with the likelihood that the number of women corporate members should show significant increases in the near future.'

Intakes into undergraduate courses in law and medicine are now about 50 per cent female, while the numbers of women reading engineering in higher education continue to increase. Although the figures are not strictly comparable with one another, the trend in the numbers of women in the Institute of Chemical Engineering also appears to be strongly upward. In 1979, only 1 per cent of their members in the United Kingdom were female, as compared with 9 per cent in Scotland in 1990; since Scotland appears generally to lag behind England in the proportions women in professional life, this ninefold increase is probably understated.

While more women appear to be entering professional life, however, to what extent are they achieving an increasing proportion of senior posts? This question is a complex one to answer, particularly because of our finding that women in Scotland generally take longer to reach senior positions than comparable male colleagues. The changes in participation in professional and managerial occupations which we have noted above are relatively recent and are likely to take at least two decades to work fully through the system. Nevertheless, there are already some indications that women are more likely to be appointed to senior posts in the 1990s. To cite only two instances, in 1990 a number of women were appointed to university chairs in Scotland, while Jean McFadden became in 1989 the first woman to serve as president of the Convention of Scottish Local Authorities.

The broader climate is also changing. SIACE (1990) has shown that most employers now say that they are committed to implementing effective equal opportunities policies. Whereas at the beginning of the 1980s there appeared to be little interest in gender as an issue or variable in research in Scotland, there is now a growing awareness of gender as an issue (see, for example, Bamford, 1988; Gerver and Johnston, 1990; Brown, 1990 (a) and (b); Brown and Fairley, 1989) and as a variable (see McKinlay, 1989 and 1990 and a number of the publications of the Centre for Educational Sociology, University of Edinburgh). There has also been a burgeoning of concern with issues which require to be addressed if women are to play a fuller part in employment (see, for instance, Hart, 1988; Glaister, 1989; SIACE, 1990; Paterson and Fewell, 1990).

A further source of encouragement may be seen in the fact that, during the latter part of the 1980s and the beginning of the 1990s, a number of key bodies in Scotland have begun to develop policies actively to promote the role of women in positions of decision-making. Almost all local authorities now have equal opportunities policies and many are actively monitoring their effects. The Scottish Office now includes an equal opportunities unit.

The Training Agency, which becomes Scottish Enterprise in 1991, is issuing to all Local Enterprise Companies a guide to good practice in equal opportunities, and the operating contract issued to each LEC will contain a paragraph on equal opportunities. Further advice and information in this area will also be issued to LECs. Information about Training 2000, an organisation designed to improve the quality and quantity of women's training in Scotland, is also being sent to all LECs. As well as receiving such advice, LECs are being required to draw up and publicise:

> A clear policy statement on Equal Opportunities which defines its objectives in this area and indicates how they are to be achieved . . . Typical questions which may need to be addressed in drawing up a policy are . . .

- do the recruitment sources and methods of selection used by local training providers give fair access to all groups in the population? . . .

- are staff adequately trained to avoid discrimination and deliver training in a manner suited to the client group?

- are there adequate monitoring and evaluation procedures built in to show whether and how objectives are achieved?

There have also been positive developments in voluntary and educational organisations. For instance, aware that the large majority of women in active membership of the Church is not reflected in the Church courts and committees, the General Assembly of the Church of Scotland in 1986 invited Presbyteries to plan for a fairer representation of women in their membership and urged the appointment of more women elders; it recognised the imbalance in representation between men and women as an 'obvious defect' (Church of Scotland, 1986).

Within the academic world, the Committee of Vice-Chancellors and Principals during 1990 consulted about a draft code of practice for equal opportunities in employment in universities. Recommendations included making efforts to increase the number of women in senior academic posts, considering flexible working arrangements and career-break schemes, ensuring that recruitment staff are trained in equal opportunities, taking full advantage of those sections of the Sex Discrimination Act 1975 which allows for positive action, and regular reporting on the implementation of equal opportunities policies. Meanwhile, perhaps as a pointer to the future, the first female law professors in Scotland were appointed to the University of Glasgow in 1990.

And what next? Inevitably, much will depend on the political climate of the 1990s. When asked by telephone in 1990 to outline their policies about female candidates, the Conservative Party in Scotland and the Scottish National Party both said that they do not have any policy about the representation of women either within the parties as a whole or as political candidates. By contrast, the Labour Party at its annual conference in Dunoon in 1990 recognised that 'real progress in women's representation will be made where there is external pressure through legislation on political parties to increase women's representation.' It recommended specific dates at which targets for female representation should be achieved: by 1992 all party committees should be composed of at least 25 per cent women; by 1994 at least 40 per cent of senior Party posts and by 1999 at least 40 per cent of Parliamentary candidates should be women. They also agreed to set comparable targets for local government. Unfortunately, the information which we requested from the Liberal Democrats did not arrive in sufficient time for inclusion.

As well, professional bodies in Scotland are now starting directly to try to increase public awareness of the potential of women to play a more significant role in professions and at senior level. During the autumn of 1990, the Law Society ran a series of advertisements designed to change public perceptions of solicitors; some of these advertisements highlight the fact that about half of younger solicitors are now female. For the Royal Institution of Chartered Surveyors, Cuckow (1990) asks: 'Will the numbers of women continue to grow? I believe that this depends on the attitude of employers in all sectors and the degree of success that the RICS achieves in changing the perception of the general public to the profession as a whole.'

Formal statements by government representatives also increasingly draw attention to the need for employers to take more seriously the potential of their female staff. Thus, welcoming the establishment of Training 2000, Ian Lang, Minister of State in the Scottish Office said:

> As yet all too few employers are making sufficient effort to develop the full potential of their female employees, or, indeed, to look for ways of modifying traditional work patterns so as to make it easier for women to join or remain in the workforce. They will undoubtedly be the losers, compared to those firms which do make the effort. Government will continue to do what we can to change attitudes in this respect. (*Training 2000 News*, 1990)

Meanwhile, in the demographic downturn, the projected decline in the number of under twenty-fives entering the workforce in the United Kingdom is much larger in Scotland then elsewhere in the country, as the graph below shows:

Figure 33

PROJECTED DECLINE IN THE NUMBER OF UNDER TWENTY FIVES
IN THE UK LABOUR FORCE 1988-2000, BY REGION

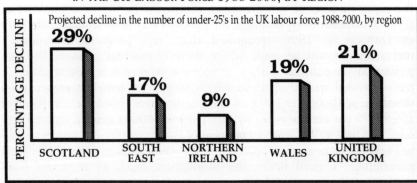

At this crucial level of economic need, therefore, the opportunities for young women first entering the labour market and women returners appear to be brighter than at any time since the last two world wars. Thus, Scottish Enterprise is enthusiastic about the prospects for women in the 1990s:

> The battle to recruit talent in Scotland will take place on two fronts. First, companies will compete for the decreasing numbers of young people available. Secondly, they will need to draw on alternative labour sources. And in this latter area there is a huge scope for development not just in relation to women currently not in employment but also in relation to women who are in work but whose skills and latent talents have not been maximised and whose training needs have not been addressed . . . The recruitment of women, their contribution and impact will all be so much greater than now. It follows that so too will be their power and influence. (Nickson, 1990)

The broader context of European developments is also likely to increase opportunities for women in Scotland to move nearer to the decision-making participation rates of their European counterparts, as Scotland grows to become more competitive with other countries in the single European market. European Community programmes are likely to have an impact on education and employment opportunities for women in Scotland. The IRIS network of training projects for women, for instance, gives priority to projects which promote training for women in occupations in which they are under-represented and in jobs for the future, while CEDEFOP has conducted work on innovatory action to change girls' and women's attitudes to career choices. The European Social Fund, EUROTECHNET, COMETT and PETRA all include a number of projects specifically for women (*Training 2000 News*, 1990).

Unreserved optimism about the future is, however, unjustified. The demographic downturn will become an upturn in the next century, and there is ample evidence of the serious downturn in women's paid employment after the First and Second World Wars. In any case, merely increasing the numbers of women recruited to particular occupations and professions does not of itself lead to their greater representation in senior positions. Adler (1990) has shown, for instance, that, despite an overall doubling of the numbers of women in the police force since the mid 1970s, the number of policewomen above the rank of constable fell from 11.2 per cent in 1971 to 5.8 per cent in 1988.

There is also now a pronounced tendency for women to form a peripheral, marginal workforce, lacking job security, good pay and, perhaps most crucially of all, promotion prospects. The failure of the United Kingdom to provide affordable high quality child care is likely to continue to provide an insuperable barrier for many women who would otherwise wish to undertake full-time education or employment. The efficacy of equal opportunities programmes is also uncertain: for example, Fitzgerald (1989) shows that, despite its equal opportunities policies, at Glasgow District Council the gap between males and females on more senior salary levels widened between 1984 and 1989. SIACE (1990) has also drawn attention to the apparent ineffectiveness in practice of many equal opportunities policies in industry in Scotland. Our interviewees rarely report much institutional interest in developing female staff; lacking such support, our interviewees have by and large apparently developed their own opportunities, albeit sometimes with the help of mentors.

Evidence also emerges from our interviews to suggest that, at present, many men in Scotland feel ill at ease when working with women as their peers or their bosses. So far, it appears as if Scottish employers who have not yet addressed the question of how most effectively to enable men and women to work together in a culture that has, until now, produced highly gendered employment patterns.

Set against such apparently bleak prospects, however, are a number of important examples of companies which have undertaken thorough development, implementation and monitoring of equal opportunities policies. For instance, British Telecom has achieved an impressive record of trends in women moving into senior positions through a high level of commitment to a fully worked out equal opportunities policy. Measures include bringing more women into engineering, increasing the numbers of women in engineering/technical management, running a women's bridging course, training all personnel assessors to recognise discrimination, providing courses to help women develop their own effectiveness and confidence, and providing role models in senior posts. They also have a policy of positive targeting of women in management positions, in which units are targeted for a minimum increase of 1 per cent in women managers per year (Sweeney, 1990).

Secondly, there is considerable evidence that it is primarily women who see gender as an issue in employment. It is therefore encouraging that a number of women recently appointed to senior posts in Scotland acknowledge their concern with gender as an issue, together with their willingness to help other women (Brown, 1990(a); MacKinnon, 1990). It is also worth noting that those organisations which tend to erect barriers against women in senior positions are likely to be less successful in attracting and retaining able women: a number of our interviewees deliberately changed employers as soon as possible after becoming aware that barriers were erected against them simply because of their gender.

Thirdly, there is evidence from our interviewees to suggest that women in senior posts bring with them many attributes likely to be helpful to the success of the companies, professions and organisations for which they work: their emphasis on innovation, their challenges to suspect methods and ideas, their preference for androgynous or gender-neutral styles, their flexible approach and their emphasis on long-term strategic thinking are all highly valuable qualities for senior positions. It is also encouraging that many of their characteristics are those traditionally highly admired in Scotland: independence, determination, a commitment to education, and, in many cases, a commitment to religious or political ideals.

Even here, however, a note of caution presses through. As Sweeney (1990) notes, the promotion of women to highly visible senior posts 'is a two edged sword . . . If successful, we can interest more women in becoming . . . managers and convince male bosses to accept them. If unsuccessful, the opposite reaction will take place, and I suspect at a *much* faster pace.' Brown (1990(c)) has also remarked on the crucial role of the first females appointed to chairs in Scottish universities: in so far as they are perceived as excellent, more substantial numbers tend to follow.

The outlook for the future, then, remains cautiously optimistic.

Names and Occupations of Interviewees

Kathleen Janette Anderson OBE — Professor and Depute Principal of Napier Polytechnic of Edinburgh

Ann Auchterlonie — Depute Director of Education, Fife Regional Council

Rt. Hon. Susan Baird — Lord Provost of Glasgow

Fiona Ballantyne — Director, Tayside and Fife Scottish Development Agency

Jean Barr — Former District Secretary, Workers' Educational Association, West of Scotland District

Lalage Bown OBE — Director and Professor of Adult and Continuing Education, University of Glasgow

Sheila Browning — Director, Total Quality Management, ICAEM Limited

Marjorie Calder — Manager, Group Marketing Services, Murray Johnstone Limited

Margaret Collins — Senior Insolvency Manager, Coopers & Lybrand Deloitte

Mary Craig — Bank Manager, TSB Scotland

Dorothy Dalton — Retired Executive Director, Scottish Community Education Council

Sandy Day — Manager, National Union of Students (Scotland)

Kate Donegan — Deputy Governor, H.M. Prison Perth

Ann Ferguson — Chairman, Fife Health Board; Director, Hatrick Bruce Limited; Board Member, Glenrothes Development Corporation

Judith George — Deputy Scottish Director, Open University in Scotland

Elisabeth Gerver — Professor of Continuing Education and Director, Centre for Continuing Education, University of Dundee

Ethel Gray CBE — Retired Founding Principal, Craigie College of Education

Lesley Hart — Head of Senior Studies Institute, University of Strathclyde

Christina Hartshorn — Enterprise Officer for Women in Scotland, University of Stirling

Anne Hepburn — Ex Chairwoman, Scottish Convention of Women
Ex National President, Church of Scotland's Woman's Guild
Catherine Hepburn — Church of Scotland Minister
Joyce Johnston — Principal, Anniesland College
Ursula Laver — Director, Public Relations Service, University of Strathclyde
Helen Liddell — Director of Personnel & Public Affairs, *Scottish Daily Record* and *Sunday Mail*
Rosemary Long — formerly Woman's Editor, *Evening Times* (now living and working in the Gambia)
Jennifer McCartney — Group Marketing Manager, Apollo Window Blinds Limited
Sheena McDonald — Journalist
Gill McIlwaine — Consultant in Public Health Medicine (Women's Health), Glasgow Royal Maternity Hospital
Margaret MacIntosh — Retired Head Teacher, Drummond Community High School
Shelagh MacKay — Finance Director, Standard Property Investment plc
Rt. Hon. Eleanor McLaughlin — Lord Provost of Edinburgh
Frances McMenamin — Advocate
Mary Marshall — Professor and Director, Dementia Services Development Centre, University of Stirling
Ann Mearns — Depute Town Clerk, Glasgow City Council
Debra Peterson — Chief Executive, California Cake & Cookie Limited
Susan Pettit — Manager, The International Stock Exchange Information Office
Isobel Anne Poole — Sheriff
Esther Roberton — Executive Director, Scottish Community Education Council
Agnes Samuel — Executive Director, Glasgow Opportunities Enterprise Trust
Joan Sandison — Retired H.M. Chief Inspector of Schools
Margaret Seymour — Managing Director, Seymour Swimming Pool Engineers
Lorna Sinclair — Publisher, Bilingual Dictionaries, Collins Publishers
Carolyn Slater — Secretary, the Royal Institution of Chartered Surveyors in Scotland
Helen Spoor — Systems Analyst, Ferranti International
Yvonne Strachan — Regional Women's Organiser, TGWU
Billie Thomson — Professor of Nursing and Head of Department of Health and Nursing, Queen Margaret College, Edinburgh
Barbara Vaughan — Marketing Co-ordinator, Angus College of Further Education; Chairman, Scottish Community Education Council
Terry Wanless — Partner, Lamont Management Consultants
Anne Watson — Information Technology Manager, Hewlett-Packard Limited
Olga Wojtas — Scottish Correspondent, *The Times Higher Education Supplement*

Appendix II

Director: Dr Archibald M Fleming MA BCom

UNIVERSITY OF
STRATHCLYDE

Continuing Eduction Centre

McChance Building, Richmond Street,
Glasgow G1 1XQ
Tel: 041-552 4400 Ext 2132/2239

LAH/AMcN   30th January, 1989
"Address"
Dear "name"
'Women: How do they manage in Scotland?'

Elisabeth Gerver, Director of the Scottish Institute of Adult and Continuing Education and I are writing a book entitled *Women: how do they manage in Scotland?* to be published by Aberdeen University Press. This book aims to investigate and analyse work, career and lifestyle strategies adopted by successful and influential women living in Scotland. It will focus on the ways in which they cope creatively with the often conflicting demands on their lives at work and at home.

The book, the first of its kind in Scotland, will be largely, although not exclusively, based on an analysis of material gathered by interviewing successful and influential women. We very much hope that you will agree to be one of those interviewed.

The time commitment on your part would be approximately 1 – 1½ hours during February/March 1989. If you wish, material from all or part of the interview would be used anonymously.

Could you please complete and return the tear-off slip below? If you agree to be interviewed, I will send you further details beforehand about the topics to be covered. Please do contact me if you wish more information before committing yourself.

As the interviews will be taking place from February, an early reply would be appreciated.

Yours sincerely,
Lesley A Hart
Co-ordinator of the Extension Programme

- -

Women: how do they manage in Scotland?
* I agree/decline to be interviewed for the above book.

Name: ....

Address: ....

....

Job Title: ....

Telephone Number: (Business) .... (Home) ....
* please delete where necessary

*Please return to: Lesley A Hart, Co-ordinator of the Extension Programme,
                      Continuing Education Centre, University of Strathclyde,
                      McCance Building, 16 Richmond Street, Glasgow G1 1XQ

Women: how do they manage in Scotland? Outline of topics and examples of questions

Section A — School Education and Family Background

SCHOOL Country and place of education. Type(s) of schools attended. Academic achievements at school. Other achievements at school. School leaving age? Qualifications on leaving school. Career thoughts at school: were these influenced by your gender? If so, how?

FAMILY Country and place of birth/upbringing. Brothers and/or sisters
BACK- — ages etc. Effects on own upbringing of having brothers and/or
GROUND sisters. Effects of place in family on upbringing. Information about parents. Jobs, lifestyle etc. Type of person you were when young — extrovert? introvert? competitive? ambitious? Ages and sex of childhood friends. Hobbies/interests when young. Childhood illnesses. Career patterns/lifestyles of brothers/sisters. In what way, if any, would your upbringing have been different if you had been a boy? Did you see yourself or were you regarded as being conventional or unconventional when young? Did you see mother or father (or someone else) as a role model? How protected/ independent were you in the family? Were you responsible for specific domestic chores? Did you travel much outwith your own environment? Were religion/politics important to you or your family?

Section B — Further and Higher Education

Details of full-time further or higher education undertaken when leaving school. Reasons for undertaking course. Career thoughts before and after course. Lifestyle during course.

Section C — Career Pattern

Details of first full-time employment. Description of career to date. Effects of marriage/divorce/children on career pattern. Mentors/role models who have influenced your career. Higher education and/or training undertaken to date. Details of career breaks. Future career thoughts. Do you think you have ever been discriminated against at work because of your sex? Have you ever been sexually harassed?

Section D — Management and Work Styles

Do you manage other people at work? If so, how many? Male or female? Are you a good manager? Do you enjoy it? How would you describe your management style? How conscious are you of gender as an issue at work? Are women managers liked/respected in the same way as male managers by their employees? Is the image of a female manager the same as the reality? Do you use new technology in your workplace? If so what and why?

Section E — Lifestyle

Domestic commitments — immediate family. Domestic commitments — extended family and friends. Sports/hobbies, interests, community work etc. How do you manage these non-work commitments? Are you happy with the balance in your life? Do you ever feel under stress? If so, how do you cope?

Section F — General Questions

If you have lived/worked outside Scotland, do you think there are intrinsically Scottish aspects which affects women's career paths? Do you think barriers still exist for women at work? What type of women do you admire most? What advice would you give a girl about to set out on her working life?

What, if any, current responsibility do you feel towards:
a)   women within your own organisation
b)   other working women outwith your organisation
c)   the women's movement

Age Group: under 30   30-39   40-49   50-59   60+

References

Acker, Sandra, and Piper, David Warren, *Is Higher Education Fair to Women?* Guildford: SRHE and NFER-Nelson, 1984.

Adler, Zsuzsanna, cited in 'A Would-Be First Among Equals', *Independent*, September 8, 1990, p 16

Baines, Alison, *Success and Satisfaction: Reconciling Women's Public and Private Selves*, London: Paladin, 1988.

Bamford, Caroline, *Gender and Education in Scotland: A Review of Research*, Edinburgh: Scottish Institute of Adult and Continuing Education, 1988.

Bartol, K M, 'Female Managers and the Quality of Working Life: the Impact of Sex Role Stereotypes', *Journal of Occupational Behaviour*, 1, 3 (July), 1980, pp 205 – 21.

BBC, *The Feminine Style* and *Wasted Assets*, videos in the series *Women in Management*, London: BBC Enterprise, 1990.

Beechey, Veronica and Whitelegg, Elizabeth, eds, *Women in Britain Today*, Milton Keynes: Open University Press, 1986.

Bem, S L, 'The Measurement of Psychological Androgyny', *Journal of Consulting and Clinical Psychology*, 42, 2, 1974, pp 155 – 62.

Bem, S L, 'Androgyny and Gender Schema Theory: a Conceptual Integration', *Nebraska Seminar on Motivation*, 32, 1985, pp 179 – 226.

Breitenbach, Esther, 'The Impact of Thatcherism on Women in Scotland', in Alice Brown and David McCrone, eds, *Scottish Government Yearbook*, Edinburgh: University Press, 1989.

Brown, Alice, 'The Context of Change: the Scottish Economy and Public Policy', in Alice Brown and John Fairley, eds, *The Manpower Services Commission in Scotland*, Edinburgh: University Press, 1989.

Brown, Sally, 'Management of Education and Social Welfare in Scotland: the Place of Women, *Scottish Journal of Adult Education*, 9, 3 (summer), 1990(a), pp 3 – 13.

Brown, Sally, 'Effective Contributions from Research to Educational Conversations: Style and Strategy', presidential address to the British Educational Research Association Annual Conference, London, 1990(b).

Brown, Sally, personal communication to Lesley Hart, September 1990(c).

Bryce, Lee, *The Influential Woman: How to Achieve Success Without Losing Your Femininity*, London: Judy Piatkus, 1989.

Buckley, Mary, and Anderson, Malcolm, eds, *Women, Equality and Europe*, London: Macmillan Press, 1988.

Burnhill, Peter, and McPherson, Andrew, 'Careers and Gender: the Expectations of Able Scottish School Leavers in 1971 and 1981', in Acker and Piper, op cit, 1984.

Byrne, Eileen, *Women and Education*, London: Tavistock Publications, 1978.

Chartered Association of Certified Accountants, facsimile message to Lesley Hart from Christine McBain, September 1990.

Church of Scotland, 'Community of Women and Men', Board of World Mission and Unity, General Assembly, Edinburgh, 1986.

Clutterbuck, D, and Devine, M, 'Having a Mentor: a Help or a Hindrance', in D Clutterbuck and M Devine, eds, *Businesswoman: Present and Future*, Basingstoke: Macmillan, 1987.

Cohen, Bronwen, 'Childcare in Europe', address to conference on child care and access, Scottish Institute of Adult and Continuing Education, Glasgow, September 1989.

Committee of Vice Chancellors and Principals of the Universities of the United Kingdom, 'Equal Opportunities in Employment in Universities', July 24, 1990.

Commission of the European Communities, 'Women in Graphics', *Women of Europe Supplements*, December 1989.

Cooper, Cary, and Davidson, Marilyn, *Women in Management: Career Development for Managerial Success*, London: William Heinemann, 1984.

Corcoran, Jennifer, 'Enforcement Procedures for Individual Complaints: Equal Pay and Equal Treatment', in Buckley and Anderson, op cit, 1988.

Coyle, Angela and Skinner, Jane, eds, *Women and Work: Positive Action for Change*, London: Macmillan Education, 1988.

Crompton, R, and Sanderson, K, 'Credentials and Careers: Some Implications of the Increase in Professional Qualifications Amongst Women', *Sociology*, 20, 1, 1986.

Cuckow, Heather, 'Encouraging Number of New Women Members', *Bulletin*, Royal Institution of Chartered Surveyors in Scotland, May 1990, p 3.

Deem, Rosemary, *All Work and No Play? A Study of Women and Leisure*, Milton Keynes: Open University Press, 1986.

Dex, Shirley, *Women's Occupational Mobility: A Lifetime Perspective*, London: Macmillan Press, 1987.

Eichler, M, *The Double Standard*, London: Croom Helm, 1980.

Fitzgerald, Jess, 'A Study of Employment Patterns and Equal Opportunities in a Scottish Local Authority', MPhil dissertation, University of Glasgow, 1989.

Fowler, Bridget, 'Women in the University of Glasgow, 1988', unpublished report for the University of Glasgow, 1989.

Game, Ann, and Pringle, Rosemary, *Gender at Work*, London: Pluto Press, 1984.

Gerver, Elisabeth, *Access Down Under: Mature Students in Australian and Scottish Universities*, Edinburgh: Scottish Institute of Adult and Continuing Education, 1990.

Gerver, Elisabeth, and Johnston, Hope, 'Is Gender Sensitivity a Problem in Scottish Educational Research Methods?', *Research Intelligence*, 36, 1990 pp 27 – 29.

Glaister, Robert, ed, *Studies of Promoted Posts*, Edinburgh: Academic Press, 1989.

Glasgow District Council, 1984 and 1989, figures cited in Fitzgerald, op cit, 1989.

Halsey, A H, 'Long, Open Road to Equality', *The Times Higher Education Supplement*, February 9, 1990, p 17.

Handy, Charles, *The Making of Managers: a Report on Management Education, Training and Development in the USA, West Germany, France, Japan and the UK*, London: National Development Office, 1987.

Hansard Society Commission, *Report on Women at the Top*, London: Hansard Society for Parliamentary Government, 1990.

Hart, Lesley, *Women's Perceived Education and Training Needs*, Edinburgh: Scottish Institute of Adult and Continuing Education, 1988.

Hennig, M, and Jardim, A, *The Managerial Woman*, London: Pan, 1979.

Henriques, Nikki, *Inspirational Women*. Wellingborough: Grapevine, 1988.

Hunt, J W, and Collins, R, *Managers in Mid Career Crisis*. Sydney: Wellington Lane, 1983.

Huppert v University Grants Commission and University of Cambridge, report of Industrial Tribunal, April 14, 1986.

Institute of Chartered Accountants in Scotland, telephone communication to Lesley Hart, September 1990.

Irvine, John, and Martin, Ben. Women in radio astronomy — shooting stars? In Jan Harding, ed. *Perspectives on Gender and Science*. London: Falmer Press, 1986.

Jensen, Jane, Hagen, Elisabeth; and Reddy, Ceallaigh, eds. *Feminisation of the Labour Force: Paradoxes and Promises*, Cambridge: Polity Press, 1988.

Jones v University of Manchester, report of Industrial Tribunal, February 16, 1989.

Jones, Liane, *Flying High: The Woman's Way to the Top*, London: Fontana, 1987.

Jowell, Roger, Brook, Lindsay and Witherspoon, Sharon. Recent trends in social attitudes. In *Social Trends 19*. London: HMSO, 1989.

Kashket, E R, Robbins, M I, Leive, L, and Huang, A S, 'Status of Women Microbiologists, *Science*, 183, 1974, pp 488-94.

Labour Party: Scottish Council, Resolution 73, annual conference, Dunoon, 1990.

MacKinlay, Andrew, *Women in Computing in Scottish Higher Education*, Edinburgh: Scottish Institute of Adult and Continuing Education, 1989(a).

MacKinlay, Andrew, 'Employment of Mature Graduates', Unpublished report for the Scottish Institute of Adult and Continuing Education, Edinburgh, 1989(b).

MacKinnon, Alistair, 'Laying Down the Law Along Parallel Lines, *Scotsman*, October 5, 1990, p 13.

Marshall, Rosalind, *Virgins and Viragos: A History of Women in Scotland from 1080 to 1980*, London: Collins, 1983.

Mehuish, Edward and Moss, Peter, *Day Care for Young Children: International Perspectives*, London: Routledge, 1990.

Miles, Rosalind. *Women and Power*. London: Macdonald, 1985.

Mitchell, Susan, *Tall Poppies: Successful Australian Women Talk*, Harmondsworth: Penguin, 1984.

Moore, Lindy, 'Invisible Scholars: Girls Learning Latin and Mathematics in the Elementary Public Schools of Scotland Before 1872', *History of Education*, 13, 2, 1984.

Mosson, Michael, address to conference on 'Efficiency and Equity', Scottish Institute of Adult and Continuing Education, June 1990.

Motowidlo, S J, 'Sex Role Orientation and Behavior in a Work Setting', *Journal of Personality and Social Psychology*, 42, 5 (May), 1982, pp 935–945.

Muir, Kate, 'Villains and the Wee Lassie Syndrome', *Observer Scotland*, January 8, 1989, p 10.

Munn, Pamela, and MacDonald, Carolyn, *Adult Participation in Education and Training*, Edinburgh: Scottish Council for Research in Education, 1988.

Nelson, Peter, *Advice and Guidance to Adults in Scotland: Training and Vocational Education*, Edinburgh: Scottish Institute of Adult and Continuing Education, 1989.

Nelson, Sarah, 'Jobs for the Boys in the Scottish Office', *Observer Scotland*, October 9, 1988. p 13.

Nickson, David, address to launch of Training 2000, Glasgow, October 1990.

Paterson, Fiona, and Fewell, Judith, eds. *Girls in their Prime: Scottish Education Revisited*, Edinburgh: Scottish Academic Press, 1990.

Petre, Jonathan, 'Pope Backs Women in their Quest for Dignity', *Daily Telegraph*, January 31, 1989, p 21.

Powell, GN, 'Sex Role Identity and Sex: an Important Distinction for Research on Women in Management', *Basic and Applied Social Psychology*, 3, 1 (March), 1982, pp 67–79.

Rapoport, R, and Rapoport, R, *Dual-Career Families Re-examined*, Oxford: Martin Robertson, 1976.

Rapoport, R, and Sierakowski, M, 'Recent Social Trends in Family and Work in Britain', *Institute of Family and Environmental Research*, London: Policy Studies Institute, 1982.

Regional Trends, 24, London: Her Majesty's Stationery Office, 1989.

Rendell, M, 'Sexist and Sexual Harassment in Education, Training and

Employment', in K Hvidtfeldt, K Jorgensen, and R Nielsen, eds, *Strategies for Integrating Women into the Labour Market*, Denmark: Women's Research Centre in Social Science, 1982.

Richards, Janet Radcliffe. *The Sceptical Feminist: A Philosophical Enquiry*, London: Routledge and Kegan Paul, 1980.

Robertson, John, 'Scotland's Third Woman QC is Named', *Scotsman*, July 28, 1989, p 3.

Sarah, E, Scott, M, and Spender, D, 'The Education of Feminists: the Case for Single-Sex Schools', in D Spencer and E Sarah, eds, *Learning to Lose*. London: Women's Press, 1980.

Scase, Richard, and Goffee, Robert, *Reluctant Managers: Their Work and Lifestyles*, London: Unwin Hyman, 1989.

SCDI, *Tomorrow's Jobs in Scotland*, Edinburgh: Scottish Council Development and Industry, 1988.

Schein, V E, 'Think Manager — Think Male', *Atlanta Economic Review*, March – April, 1976.

Scott, Gill, *Childcare and Access: Women in Tertiary Education in Scotland*, Edinburgh: Scottish Institute of Adult and Continuing Education, 1989(a).

Scott, Gill, *Families and Under-Fives: A Survey of Children Under Five and Pre-School Services in Strathclyde*, Glasgow: Glasgow College and Strathclyde Regional Council, 1989(b).

Scottish Education Department, *Scottish Examination Board Report for 1986*, Edinburgh: Scottish Education Department, 1987.

Scottish Education Department, 'Scottish Higher Education Statistics', *Statistical Bulletin* 12, Edinburgh: Scottish Education Department, August, 1990.

SIACE, *Efficiency and Equity: Training for Women for Management*, Edinburgh: Scottish Institute of Adult and Continuing Education, 1990.

Singer, J, *Androgyny: Towards a New Theory of Sexuality*, New York: Doubleday, 1976.

Slater, Carolyn, letter to Lesley Hart on women members of Royal Institution of Chartered Surveyors in Scotland, September 1990.

Social Trends, 19. London: Her Majesty's Stationery Office, 1989.

Spencer, Anne, and Podmore, David, eds, *In a Man's World: Essays on Women in Male-Dominated Professions*, London: Tavistock Publications, 1987.

Still, Leonie, *Becoming a Top Woman Manager*, Sydney: Allen and Unwin, 1988.

Strathclyde, University of, statistics on academic staff by gender, supplied courtesy of Lesley Hart, 1990.

Stirling District Council Equal Opportunities Working Group, *Positive Action Plan and Targets for Equal Opportunities in Employment, 1989 – 91*. Stirling District Council, 1989.

Sutherland, Margaret, *Women Who Teach in Universities*, Stoke on Trent: Trentham Books, 1985.

Sutherland, Margaret, 'Research About Women Returners', in David Hartley, ed, *Adult Learning in Scotland: a Review of Research and Policy*, Edinburgh: Scottish Council for Research in Education and Scottish Institute of Adult and Continuing Education, 1990.

Sweeney, Joan, address to conference on 'Efficiency and Equity', Scottish Institute of Adult and Continuing Education, Glasgow, June 1990.

Training Agency, *Developing Good Practice: Equal Opportunities*. Sheffield: Employment Department Training Agency, undated [1990].

Training 2000 News, 1, pp 1 and 7, Edinburgh: Training 2000, 1990.

Vallance, Elizabeth, 'Do Women Make a Difference? The Impact of Women MEPs on Community Equality Policy, in Buckley and Anderson, op cit, 1988.

Watson, Sophia, *Winning Women: The Price of Success in a Man's World*, London: Weidenfield and Nicolson, 1989.

Who's Who in Scotland, Ayr: Carrick Publishing, 1988.

Wickham, Ann, *Women and Training*, Milton Keynes: Open University Press, 1986.

Women in Scotland Bibliography Group, *Women in Scotland: an Annotated Bibliography*, Edinburgh: Open University in Scotland, 1988.

Yeandle, Susan, *Women's Working Lives: Patterns and Strategies*, London: Tavistock Publications, 1984.

Index